THE GREAT BOOK OF TENNIS

OF TENNIS

Interesting Facts and Sports Stories

Sports Trivia Vol.6

Bill O'Neill

DON'T FORGET YOUR
FREE BOOKS

CONTENTS

INTRODUCTION

Like many modern games, there are origins long ago. In the case of tennis, French monks, it seems, were the founders of the game that is enjoyed today. "Real tennis" was played indoors, but once the norm was outside, and it did depend a little on the weather.

The original name included the word "lawn", which confirmed that point, and at the start of the major championships often described as "Grand Slams", all four were played on grass. It is clear that the game in the early decades was largely played by wealthy people. There was no chance of funding good grass courts for ordinary people, and even into the middle of the 20th Century, some future champions needed help to develop even early glimpses of talent.

The game was purely amateur, and that was another obstacle to ordinary people involving themselves in the game. As tennis became organised with proper rules and agreed court dimensions, competition began with the defending champion having the luxury of waiting for the winner of the knockout stages to give someone the right to challenge him or her. Today's champions would have loved the luxury of a single appearance which contrasts with two-week competitions with 128 entries in the main singles draw.

This book is divided into seven Chapters, starting with an introduction to the game. The next two chapters are devoted to men's tennis, the first going from the beginning and through to the Open Era with those whose careers came either side largely dealt with in Chapter 2. The same applies to the women, covered in Chapters 4 and 5. The doubles has a chapter to itself, with in the early days many of the players still playing in all three events. That is less of a case today with the really top men's players concentrating purely on singles. The final chapter looks at developments across the world game and takes a look at the careers of some good amateurs who turned professional before the Open Era and did not really feature much again at the Grand Slams, mostly through retirement and age.

Hopefully, you will enjoy the book and come away having a greater appreciation of this wonderful game, tennis.

CHAPTER 1
ORIGINS, RULES & STRUCTURE

The Origins of Tennis

There are pictures of a game that looks something like tennis that date back to the Ancient Empires of the Egyptians, Greeks, and Romans. Arabic text suggests that the town of Tinnis on the River Nile might have given its name to the game.

There are no other references to the sport for many centuries, however, not until stories of French monks emerged, playing a game in which they used their hands to strike the ball either against the wall of the monastery or over a rope which was strung across the courtyard. The argument proposed by people in France was the game took the word "tenez" in French, meaning "take this", reference to a player addressing an opponent. At the time, this game was called "jeu de palme" meaning hand game.

Over the years, people started to wear gloves and then use a very basic form of racket. The ball was hard, cork or wool, wrapped in cloth or leather, and slowly, it looked something like today's baseball. The game was played indoors. Walls were still employed. The nobility soon took an interest, and more and more courts were built in the 13th Century with the game spreading to Tudor England.

Rackets were commonly used by 1500, and the game, now known as "real tennis" can be played today on a court in Hampton Court. The ball is hit off the walls of a narrow room (court) that has a series of different angles that test the receiver in terms of the angles that the ball will take, and therefore players need to anticipate where the ball will be coming in order to hit it. There was a net at the end of the court that was 5 feet high at the sides and 3 feet in the middle.

The popularity of the game faded until the middle of the 19th Century when Charles Goodyear invented the vulcanization of rubber, meaning that bouncy rubber balls could be made.

An outdoor game emerged soon afterwards, and it required new rules; there were no walls, just the net. In 1874, Major Walter C. Wingfield patented the equipment and rules for a game that closely resembles the game of today. Tennis courts soon appeared in the USA. The court was a different shape than the one of today, but changes were to follow, with the All England Club holding a tournament in 1877 on a rectangular court rather than the one that had looked like an "egg timer", narrow close to the net and then widening out towards the ends.

Court Dimensions

The dimensions of a tennis court are laid out in imperial measurement, feet rather than metres. A court is 78 feet long and 36 feet wide, but that includes the lines that are used only in doubles, not singles. The width of the court for singles is 27 feet. There is a further line across the court to the singles' line, 21 feet from the net on each side. That creates the space into which the player serving the ball must hit that ball to commence a point.

The 27 feet width is divided equally with the line going from the net to this "service line", so two boxes, each 21 ft. x 13.5 ft., become the target for the server. Two small lines on the base line create two imaginary halves of the court, halves that measure 78 feet in length and 18 feet in width.

The net that is stretched across the court is 3.5 feet high at the posts at either side and 3 feet in the centre. A cord, actually a strap, 2 inches deep, is sewn on to the top of the net as a means of controlling the net's height. The cord comes into play of course; if a serve hits the cord and still lands in the service area, a "let" is played. Otherwise, if the ball goes into the opponent's half, it remains in play, and that can often give an advantage to one or other player depending upon the effect the cord has had on the ball.

The Tennis Racket

The game of tennis was once played with something that was little more than a plank of wood. Major Walter C. Wingfield was responsible for the first one in 1874, and for years there was little alternative.

The use of a laminated wooden racket is attributed to Rene Lacoste, just after the end of World War II. The first steel racket in 1968 changed things dramatically. It was a favourite with Jimmy Connors, who was extremely successful with it.

By now, there was a significant market for rackets, and just a few years later, an aluminium racket was introduced, lighter but equally as strong. The "Weed" brand was also oversized, and many saw that as an improvement as well. The bestseller though was Howard Head's " Prince" that came out a year later.

In 1980, with wood now obsolete, major brands introduced graphite rackets, which leading players immediately took up. Inevitably, there were further developments with one of those, the first "widebody" racket offering more power.

Tungsten and titanium have been used to add power and strength while also make rackets lighter. As in many of today's popular professional sports, equipment is big business with the market for casual tennis players worldwide.

Tennis Balls

The tennis balls you know today have their origins in the 1920s. They were pressurized and covered with felt to improve their aerodynamics. The important quality was their bounce, and to help retain that, they were stored in sealed cans or tubes. The ITF has strict rules about bounciness, and it involves a test. A ball dropped from 254 cm (100 inches) on to a concrete surface must bounce back more than 135 cm but not more than 147 cm. Tests have to be done under uniform conditions, which include temperatures of 20C, 60% humidity, and 102Pa atmospheric pressure.

The diameter of the ball has a range between 65.41mm and 68.58mm and 56 – 59.4 gm. The standard colour of yellow was introduced in 1972 to improve their visibility.

The Rules of Tennis

The object of the game is to hit the ball, on the full or after it has bounced just once into the opponent's half of the court in the hope that he or she cannot return it. A point is scored when either side cannot return the ball within the marked court or hits the net with the ball.

A court can have a variety of surfaces—grass, clay, hard surface, and carpet.

The scoring system is one in which a player who serves must win four points to register a game and six games to register a set. The player receiving the service can also win the game, known as breaking service. A set must be won by two clear games, but in the modern game, there is a tie-breaker at 6 – 6 whereby one or the other of the players must win by two clear points in a 13th game. The service order starts with the player whose turn it is to serve having one initial service. From there, each player serves twice until one player has seven points and a two-shot lead. There is no restriction as to how many points are played. The only stipulation is that one player wins the set once he or she has a two point lead and a minimum of seven points.

The score in the regular games in a set are unique: 15, 30, 40, and game. A 40 – 40 is called "deuce" and then the game can only be won with a two-point margin, the first being "advantage." The score returns to "deuce" if the opponent wins the next point after an advantage is gained.

In professional tennis, the tournament can decide the format. Women never play more than best of three sets, though men in Grand Slams, and occasionally elsewhere in finals play best of five sets.

Players take turns serving, and for each point, the server has just two attempts to get the ball in play before losing the point. If the serve hits the net cord yet still falls into the correct area, it is retaken without penalty.

Tennis as Recreation

It may seem obvious to say, but people could only play tennis if they had access to facilities. There were public courses but a limited number of clubs where people could play. It was a fairly elitist sport that required local authorities to maintain public facilities if they were to be worth playing on. These facilities were rarely grass surfaces simply because of the issue of maintenance, yet even though Wimbledon would never desert grass, Melbourne and the Australian Open did, and there are a limited number of grass tournaments, virtually all played in the short period before Wimbledon.

Multipurpose sports halls are often marked out these days for several sports—tennis, badminton, basketball, 5-a-side soccer, etc. Such facilities are still not as plentiful as sports-loving people would like, and tennis is not favoured by the need for proper facilities.

There have been eras when countries have looked to tennis because of national success. There is no doubt that the era of Australian players through the 50s, 60s, and part of the 70s came along because of youngsters taking up a popular national sport. The same could be said about Sweden after Bjorn Borg's success, and the Czech women that seemed to be coming off a conveyor belt during the Open Era in the latter part of the 20th Century.

International Lawn Tennis Federation (ILTF)

It became clear that tennis needed organization. It was growing worldwide, though with the exception of South Africa and Australasia, predominantly in Europe. In a conference in Paris in 1913, the ILTF was founded with a view to develop a uniform structure to the game.

Initially, three countries decided not to accept voting shares, and they included the USA and Canada. The War halted proceedings, and it was not until 1923 that the "Rules of Tennis" were adopted with today's Four Grand Slams recognized as Official Championships.

The ILTF gradually became recognized as the controlling authority in the world, and with the invasion of France early in World War II, the headquarters were switched to London where they still remain today.

The debate on amateur and professional status was a topic that received attention. The original idea was that an amateur could only take expenses for eight weeks, otherwise he or she could not retain gainful employment. In the 1930s, a number of the top players turned professional and played in front of fairly large crowds. There was little at stake, and the pool of players was small, so the matches would ultimately be seen as exhibition games. Whether that circuit would have grown and been sustained no one will know. World War II was one of the reasons why it wasn't.

In 1946, there were 23 members as activities resumed, with some countries temporarily removed as a consequence of the War. In 1951, that was extended to 210 days.

The Federation Cup was launched for Women in 1963, the 50th Anniversary of the formation of the ILTF. Remember, the male equivalent, the Davis Cup, had been run since 1900, though not under the control of the ILTF.

Pressure was building in tennis; how could an amateur play for 210 days for expenses? In 1968, the "Open Era" was announced following a meeting of 47 countries in Paris. World Championship Tennis (WCT) would run in opposition to the ILTF circuit.

The Formative Years of Professionalism

At the ILTF AGM in 1971, it was decided that no tennis player contracted to the WCT could play in an event organized by a national association, that means the ones now regarded as the Grand Slams. The consequence was that John Newcombe could not defend his Wimbledon title in 1971. That was resolved the following year, while in the women's game, peace was declared between the ILTF, National Associations, and the newly formed Virginia Slims Tour.

There was one more major problem which resulted in the 1973 Wimbledon Championship being competed for by a field missing most of the top players. The Association of Tennis Professionals (ATP) decided to support Nikki Pilic, who had been given a suspension by the ILTF for missing a Davis Cup tie.

The ATP, ILTF, and the National Associations formed the Grand Prix Committee which in 1975 became the Men's International Professional Tennis Council with equal representation. The women had an equivalent immediately.

Something that some people regard as sad was that the ILTF became the ITF, dropping "lawn" from its title in 1977.

ATP

One of the first things that the ATP did when it was formed in 1972, prime movers being Jack Kramer and Cliff Drysdale, was to introduce a ranking system as the best way to decide entries into tournaments. The first list came out in September 1973 and continues to this day. Up until 1989, the tennis circuit was run by the Men's Tennis Council, with representatives from the ATP, ITLF, and tournament directors. Tennis certainly progressed under its guidance, but players began to realise they needed more control, and that evolved with a new tennis circuit, the ATP Tour, to which the vast majority of the World's top 100 players signed contracts for playing in 1990.

While the Grand Slams have 128 competitors playing over two weeks, the weekly ATP Events are much smaller. There are many tennis players aspiring to reach the main competitions and several lower level events around the world where they can make a living, but these players going no higher up the structure will never be millionaires.

WTA

As an illustration of how many tennis players an association represents, the Women's Tennis Association now has 2,500 members in 100 countries competing for $146m. There are 54 events in 30 countries on the 2018 calendar as well as the Grand Slams.

The origins of the association also date back to the 1970s, and particularly to Billie Jean King. The Virginia Slims Series had nine original signatories, with Houston hosting the first event in September 1970. For 1971, there were 19 tournaments and a total purse of just over $300,000. The WTA was born of a meeting of 60 professionals just before Wimbledon in 1973, and the US Open agreed to equal prize money.

The first ranking system came in 1975, and by the end of the decade there were 250 women professionals and 47 global events. The WTA Players Association merged with the Women's Tennis Council to form the WTA Tour.

Wimbledon

Wimbledon is the oldest tennis tournament in the world, the first tournament being held in 1877. It is the third in the calendar year and is run by the All England Lawn Tennis and Croquet Club in Wimbledon. It has always been played on grass and now has two of its eighteen courts, Centre and No. 1 with retractable roofs. The first tournament was just men's singles, but that has been expanded to men and women, singles and doubles, mixed doubles, juniors, and veterans, as well as wheelchair events. There were no Championships during the War years. The first prize money was awarded in 1968, with equal prize money relatively recent in 2007. The 1968 winner received £2,000, but by 2011 that exceeded £1m. Wimbledon has maintained the requirement for predominantly white clothing despite that changing elsewhere in the world. However, manufacturer's logos are now easily identified on players.

Australian Open

The Lawn Tennis Association of Australasia was formed in 1904 by the six State tennis bodies in Australia and the body running the game in New Zealand. The following year, the Australasian Men's Championships were held in Melbourne. The following year, it switched to New Zealand. When the ILTF was formed a few years later, it was designated as what is now usually referred to as a Grand Slam event. It is played early in the year, and the Open remains the first of the four Grand Slams in the calendar year. It was initially played on grass, but in 1988, it changed to hard court. There are five senior events, boys and girls, and a Masters. The women's event dates back to 1922, incidentally.

French Open

The first French Championship was held in 1891 and was won by a Briton who was resident in Paris.

At the time, it was only for French residents. The women began in 1897. It was not until 1925 that the event became truly international, though of course it was for amateurs only. French tennis was fairly strong at that time. In 1925, the event was held for the first time at Roland Garros, its current home. The Men's Trophy is known as "Coupe de Mousquetaires" in honour of the four French players nicknamed the Four Musketeers for their exploits in winning the 1928 Davis Cup in Philadelphia: Rene Lacoste, Jacques Brugnon, Jean Borotra, and Henri Cochet.

US Open

The US Open Championship developed out of two separate tournaments, the Men's that was held at Newport in 1881, and the 1887 Women's played at Philadelphia Cricket Club. Women's Doubles were held in 1889 (mixed was a year earlier.) American residents were the only players allowed in the early days. The Championships were played on grass until 1975, when for a short time they were played on clay. From 1978, the surface has been hard court.

World Championships

The ATP and WTA Tours both hold an end of season tournament for the best eight players of the year. It does not necessarily mean that the winners are ranked No. 1 from that point because points are allocated throughout the season, and someone who has a fine season needs to defend his or her status the following year. This is a simple way to explain why Rafael Nadal remains at No. 1 after the Australian Open in January 2018, but he now has a large number of points to defend to stay there. Roger Federer missed the clay court season last year and has no points to defend.

FACTS & FIGURES

1. The US Open was called the Patriotic Tournament in 1917 during the First World War.

2. The strings of tennis racket have been made out of a cow and sheep guts.

3. The French Open is named after the hosting stadium, which in turn remembers a First World War I pilot, Roland Garros.

4. Tennis first appeared in the Olympics in 1896 but was dropped after the 1924 games. It was a demonstration sport in 1968 and 1984, then re-introduced for the 1988 Olympic Games.

5. There are over 200 ball boys and ball girls who collect tennis balls during Wimbledon. It takes eight hours training a week for four months to be ready for the tournament.

6. Wimbledon used to have a challenge round system (the defending champion qualified for following year's final) between 1877 and 1921.

7. The youngest player to win a match in the US Open was Vincent Richards in 1918; he was 15 years, 5 months, and 8 days.

8. A five set women's final used to be played at the US Open between from 1887 and 1901.

9. In the US Open, between 1884 and 1911 for men and 1887 to 1918 for women, a challenge round system (the defending champion qualified for the following year's final) was the format.

10. The oldest winner of the US Open was Bill Larned; 38 years, 8 months, and 3 days in 1911, when he won his 7th and last title.

11. 37,247 buckets of hot chips, 37,305 BBQ sausages, 2,500kg of curry, and 164,416 ice creams were sold during the Australian Open 2006.

12. The Women's singles winner of the French Open receives the Coupe Suzanne Lenglen, a former French tennis star.

13. No one is certain where the expression "love" comes from in tennis (it represents zero). Some think it was the French for egg, "l'ouef".

14. Henry "Bunny" Austin became the first player to wear shorts at Wimbledon in 1932.

15. Women used to wear full length dresses when playing in the Wimbledon tournament.

16. Twenty-four tons of strawberries are consumed every year at the Wimbledon Championships.

17. Other than an umpire and a net cord official, each game requires someone on each of the lines to decide whether a ball is in or out. That adds up to ten line officials. These days, they are helped by the "hawkeye" technology which players can use to appeal a decision.

18. The least popular position amongst line judges is the centre line because that can be in the direct line of a speedy service.

19. George VI played in the men's doubles event at Wimbledon in 1926; he was merely Price Albert at the time.

20. Jimmy Connors is the only player to win the US Open on three different surfaces: grass, clay, and hard court.

TRIVIA QUESTIONS

1. How wide is a single tramline at the side of a tennis court?

   A. 3 feet
   B. 3.5 feet
   C. 4 feet
   D. 4.5 feet
   E. 5 feet

2. Which Grand Slam Trophy is known as the "Coupe de Mousquetaires"?

   A. The French Men's
   B. The French Women's
   C. Wimbledon
   D. US Open
   E. Australian Open

3. When was "lawn" dropped by the ILTF, renaming itself ITF?

   A. 1972
   B. 1974
   C. 1975
   D. 1976
   E. 1977

4. Which USA University tennis team played in the first Davis Cup?

    A. Yale

    B. UCLA

    C. Harvard

    D. Arizona State

    E. University of Texas.

5. How many points clear must a player be to win an individual game within a match?

    A. 1

    B. 2

    C. 3

    D. 4

    E. 5

Answers

1. D
2. A
3. E
4. C
5. B

CHAPTER 2

MEN FROM AMATEUR
TO PROFESSIONAL

The amateur game of tennis only permitted players to take a very limited amount of expenses. The implications were obvious. Someone who wanted to play in a number of tournaments needed the means to do so. That does not necessarily devalue the achievement of winning a competition. However, if you also consider that Grand Slams involved a challenge round for some years, the odds were very much stacked towards an elite in the very early days.

The game was nowhere near as organised as it is today. The game did not have the true global appeal that it has today, and given the amateur regulations, it was not a realistic prospect for someone from a poor family to take up the game seriously and develop into a top player without a great deal of legitimate support.

There are many famous names that played purely as amateurs and a few whose careers spanned the end of the amateur game and the beginning of the "Open Era." Here is a selection of fifteen who certainly deserve mention.

William Renshaw

William Renshaw was the first player to win seven Wimbledon Men's singles, six of which were consecutive, between 1881 and 1886, and that has never been beaten. He first played at Wimbledon in 1880, and his last appearance was in 1890.

He won the Doubles five times as well, 1884 to 1886, 1889 and 1890 playing with his twin brother, Ernest, whom he beat in three of the finals. His lone final defeat was in 1888 against Herbert Lawford, whom he had beaten in the 1884 final.

He was the first President of the Lawn Tennis Association.

William A Larned

Larned won his first Grand Slam event at 28, the US in 1901 when he beat Beals Wright. He went on the win the Title seven times, the last in 1911 when he was 38, which means even today, he is the oldest-ever US Champion. He played in four successive finals, 1900-1903, and in eleven in all.

When a student at Cornell University, he won the 1892 Intercollegiate singles Championship.

He played for years in the Davis Cup Team and was captain four times. His singles wins helped the US win the Cup in 1902, and they reached the finals in 1903, 1905, 1908, 1909, and 1911.

He retired in 1911, when his rheumatism became too much of a hindrance.

Anthony Wilding

Kiwi Anthony Wilding won four Wimbledon titles between 1910 and 1913, having taken the Australian title previously in 1906 and 1909. He had begun as a 17-year-old in 1901 by winning the Canterbury Championship on South Island, New Zealand, and made his Wimbledon debut three years later.

His first Wimbledon success, having beaten Beals Wright in the Draw, was against Arthur Gore in the Challenge Round; the first New Zealand name on the trophy. He then won three more times but lost to his Doubles partner, Norman Brookes, to stop his winning a fifth.

He had several other wins, on clay at the World Hard Court Championships, grass at the World Lawn Tennis Championships, and wood in the World Covered Court Championship.

In Doubles, he and Brookes won Wimbledon Titles in 1907 and 1914, while he won the 1908 and 1910 Titles with Brit Josiah Ritchie. Wilding and Brookes played together in the Australasia (Australia and New Zealand) Davis Cup team, winning in 1907, 1908, 1909, and 1914, each time against the USA.

At the start of the First World War I, he joined the Royal Marines as a Captain in the battlefields of France and was killed at the Battle of Aubers Ridge in 1915 at the age of 31.

Bill Tilden

William Tatem Tilden II, "Big Bill," was the dominant figure in men's tennis between 1920 and 1926. He won six US National Championship Men's singles titles in a row and Wimbledon twice, in 1920 and 1921. He didn't play at Wimbledon then until 1927, losing at the semi-final stage for three years in a row before winning a third title in 1930. In addition, he won thirteen straight Davis Cup matches, with the United States taking seven consecutive titles.

He won five men's doubles titles and four mixed doubles championships. Tilden played as an amateur from 1912 until 1931 and then turned professional to play some of the other famous names of the 30s who did likewise.

He finally retired in 1946 with estimated earnings of $500,000 and impressive statistics including a 78-1 single season match streak in 1925.

Rene Lacoste

Lacoste was part of a golden age in French tennis in the 1920s and early 1930s. He didn't begin to play tennis until he was 15. His career was brief, yet by the age of 24, he had won eleven Majors, seven singles, and four doubles, as well as being part of the outstanding French Davis Cup side.

He got the nickname "crocodile" which he was to use in his

famous clothing brand. He had been promised a crocodile skin suitcase if he won an important game; remember these were amateur days. He was very tenacious on court, so perhaps it was a suitable name?

He played from the baseline, and had a range of shots while also varying his pace. He won the French three times, 1925, 1927, and 1929, Wimbledon in 1925 and 1928, and the US in successive seasons, 1926 and 1927. In this period, finals were often contested between Frenchmen, with Borotra Lacoste's fierce competitor when it came to titles. However, he twice beat Tilden in Grand Slam finals as well. Borotra was Lacoste's Doubles partner, winning three French Titles and one at Wimbledon.

His health wasn't great in those days, and he retired in 1929, launching his clothing brand four years later. In later life, he invented the steel tennis racquet in 1963 that was ultimately to lead to the end of wood. His daughter was US Open champion in 1967, playing as an amateur.

Henri Cochet

Cochet was born in Lyon, the son of the greenkeeper at the city's tennis club. Despite being only 5 feet 6 inches, he was powerful and quick. As well as being part of the "Four Musketeers" (René Lacoste, Jacques Brugnon, and Jean Borotra) that dominated the Davis Cup, he won five French Titles between 1922 and 1932. During that time, he won two

Wimbledons, 1927 and 1929, as well as the US in 1928.

He beat Bill Tilden in the Wimbledon semi-final in 1927 from being two sets and 5 – 1 down. He then won six straight games to take the 3rd 7 – 5 and won the next two sets as well. He saved 6 match points in the final against Borotra at 5 – 2 down in the 5th but won five games in a row to win 7 – 5.

He and Jacques Brugnon won the French three times and Wimbledon twice, as well as silver in the 1924 Olympics. He won mixed at the French twice, as well as the 1927 US. In 1933, he turned professional but was re-instated as an amateur in 1945.

He played around the world in a 25-year career and was still teaching tennis into his 70s.

Jean Borotra

Borotra was part of a wonderful era of French men's tennis. He was Basque, born in Biarritz, and played in France's dominant spell in the Davis Cup between 1927 and 1932. His own record in the Cup was 36 wins from 54 games.

He won 21 major championships across singles, doubles and mixed. He was known for his style and charm on the court, wearing a range of berets and when he ended up in the stands after chasing a wide shot, and always kissed the nearest lady's hand.

His singles Grand Slam successes were Wimbledon, in 1924

beating Lacoste and 1926 against Howard Kinsey, the Australian in 1928, the 1931 French after it became a Grand Slam Open Championship (in 1924, he won the French when only French residents could play.) His US final was in 1926 when he lost to Lacoste. His four final defeats were all to Frenchmen, Lacoste twice and Cochet twice.

He won five Doubles in Paris, three with Lacoste who partnered him to one of his three Wimbledon Championships. He won in Australia in 1928 and also won the mixed there once, with further wins in the US (1), Wimbledon (1), and France (3).

Baron Gottfried von Cramm

Long before Boris Becker, Germany had a tennis hero. Tall, blond, with green eyes, the Baron played elegant tennis, and it produced five major titles across the three games. He was popular among his rivals, and historians of the game still talk about his 1937 Davis Cup match against Don Budge which the American won 8 – 6 in the 5th for a 3 – 2 USA victory. Two years earlier, he had said he had touched the ball before it was returned by his partner to win. The point was given to the USA, who went on to win the set 8 – 6, and ultimately the Cup. He stood on his honour but was not popular with others in Germany for doing so.

He appeared in seven Grand Slam singles finals and won two French Championships in 1934 and 1936. Both of von Cramm's victories went to five sets, defeating Crawford 6-4, 7-9, 3-6, 7-5, 6-3 in 1934 and Fred Perry in 1936, 6-0, 2-6, 6-2, 2-6, 6-0, after having lost to Perry in the 1935 final. He lost twice more to Perry at Wimbledon and to Budge at Wimbledon and the US.

He played 111 Davis Cup matches for Germany and won six German Championships Titles, the last at 40 years old in 1949. Von Cramm with partner Henner Henkel won two Grand Slam Doubles Titles, the French, and the US, as well as the mixed in 1933 at Wimbledon with Hilde Krahwinkel.

Ellsworth Vines

Vines was a shy teenager yet developed into a confident man whose tennis prowess should never be underrated. Born in California, he won his first US Title at 19 in 1931, and the following year he retained it with a straight sets win against Henri Cochet. That same year, he had won Wimbledon beating Bunny Austin in straight sets in the final.

He lost in the final the following year but won the 1933 Australian Doubles and the US mixed with Keith Gledhill and Elizabeth Ryan respectively.

His Davis Cup record in the two years of playing was an impressive 13 – 3.

He turned professional in 1934 and began to dominate winning five titles in no times, Wembley between 1934 and 1936, the French on clay in 1935, and the US in 1939. His game against

Fred Perry in 1939 at Madison Square Garden attracted over 17,500 spectators.

He retired the following year and took up golf, turning professional in 1942. He had a few wins, reached the semi-finals of the PGA when it was still match play, and played in the Masters with Bobby Jones.

Don Budge

History was made in 1938. Don Budge became the first man in history to win the four Grand Slam Championships in the same season. Bill Tilden won more titles, but many judged Budge to be the more complete player. He had a fine service and strong forehand with a backhand that had few equals.

The previous season, Budge had won all three Titles at Wimbledon, and he repeated that in 1938. He didn't lose a set throughout, beating Bunny Austin for the loss of just four games in the final. He won the US Open treble in 1938, having just taken two titles the year before; he lost in the doubles final in 1937.

He turned professional in 1939, making his debut in front of 17,725 spectators at Madison Square Garden. He had winning records against all the prominent professionals at the time; Ellsworth Vines, Bill Tilden and Fred Perry. He took the US Professional title in 1942, defeating Bobby Riggs, who famously challenged and lost to Billy Jean King years later. He joined the

US Air Force shortly afterwards.

Fred Perry

Fred Perry remains the only Briton to win all four Grand Slam events. He won Wimbledon three years in a row in the mid-1930s, and it was to be 77 years before another Brit, Andy Murray, was able to keep the Trophy in the UK when he won in 2013. Perry had been world table tennis champion in 1929, but it is for tennis and later his sporting brand for which he is best remembered.

Perry was born in 1909 in Stockport, Cheshire, into a working class family. The family moved to Ealing, and his father became MP for Kettering in 1929.

He concentrated on tennis after that table tennis win in Budapest and won the US Open in 1933, as well as then winning three of the four Grand Slams the following season. It was in 1935, with a win in Paris, that he completed his personal Grand Slam. It was Wimbledon and the US in 1936 before he turned professional. His straight sets win at Wimbledon against Baron Gottfried von Cramm for the loss of just two games took just 45 minutes. Despite his success, he wasn't popular amongst the officials of the All England Club who were supposed to make a presentation of a tie to him when winning the Title. It was merely left for him to collect.

It wasn't until the 50th Anniversary of a Wimbledon success that he was truly recognised by the All-England Club whose treatment of him during his successes was off-hand. He moved to the USA and became an American citizen as well as a successful coach and businessman.

Ken Rosewall

The Australian Open in Melbourne is often played in high temperatures. When Ken Rosewall became the oldest Grand Slam winner in the Open Era at 37 in 1972, the temperature was above 100 F. His opponent Mal Anderson was actually 36; where were the youngsters?

Rosewall's career spanned the period when only amateurs could contest the Grand Slams through to the Open Era. Rosewall had beaten Arthur Ashes to take the Title the previous year as well, not losing a set throughout.

He first won the Australian Championship at 18, in 1953, and it was 21 years later when he played in his last Grand Slam finals, losing both at Wimbledon to Jimmy Connors, and then in the US Open. His record was eight Grand Slam singles, nine doubles, and a single mixed.

His first French Title was in 1953 and his last 1972; his first US 1956 and last 1970. It was a remarkable career. He was still ranked No. 2 in the world at the age of 40, and at 43 defeated Ille Nastase to win the Tokyo Gunze Open.

He had begun to play tennis at the tender age of 3. He was

naturally left-handed, but his father switched him to a "righty". After three Grand Slams, he turned professional in 1957, winning the professional equivalents of the Grand Slams; eight French, five Wembley and two US. As soon as the Open Era arrived, he won the French, beating his regular rival, Rod Laver, in four sets. It was Laver at his peak that was a significant reason why he could not take the only thing missing from his CV, the Wimbledon Championship.

He won nine doubles majors, at all four Grand Slam events with five of those partnered by Lew Hoad, while he won the US mixed in 1956 with Margaret Osborne duPont.

He first represented Australia in the Davis Cup at eighteen in 1953, and was in four Cup winning sides, the last in 1973.

Rod Laver

Rod Laver's record of two calendar Grand Slams is unlikely ever to be matched. He turned professional for a period but was able to return to the Grand Slams to complete his second in 1969. He had over 200 tournament titles but remained utterly modest and currently enjoys watching today's stars in the Rod Laver Arena in Melbourne at the Australian Open.

He was the first to reach $1m in prize money, and in total reached $1.5m, which is insignificant in modern day terms, such is the popularity of the game. Laver made a great contribution towards that in the 60s.

His Grand Slam singles record reads eleven, but it was from only sixteen attempts. When he turned professional after his first Calendar Grand Slam, he had six in all, the extra two being the Australian and Wimbledon. Returning in the Open Era, he won Wimbledon again in 1968, and his second calendar Grand Slam in 1969. In addition, he won seven doubles and two mixed, with only the USA missing from his CV.

Laver was born in Rockhampton, Australia, to a cattle rancher and a mother who was a good tennis player. He started tennis at six and at thirteen lost the Central Queensland Junior final to his older brother, Bob.

In 1953, Laver left school to concentrate on tennis and won the 1956 US junior championship. He had 54 amateur titles from then until 1962 when he turned professional. A left-hander, the strength in his left arm and wrist was easy to see; they were bigger than the right equivalents due to his hard work.

He lost his first Wimbledon final in 1959 to Alex Olmedo but took the Australian Title the following year. After the 1962 Grand Slam, Laver purportedly signed a contract for $100,000 to play professionally.

From 1964, he won the US Pro five times in six years, added the Wembley Pro, the French Pro, and US Pro titles later, the professional Grand Slam and won 69 tournaments in all as a pro, nineteen in 1967. The Open Era returned, and so did Laver with five of the next seven Grand Slams.

Laver won the Davis Cup with Australia five times, four before he first turned professional and a fifth in 1973.

Roy Emerson

While Roy Emerson struggled to get the better of Laver, he still emerged to win twelve Grand Slam singles and sixteen doubles with Neale Fraser and often with partner Fred Stolle, whom he regularly beat in singles finals. He was born on a dairy farm in Queensland. Nine of those 28 Grand Slam events were in Australia, whom he helped to eight Davis Cups between 1959 and 1967 with a singles record of 14 — 4. His record six Australian Titles has since been matched and his twelve singles titles were a record until Pete Sampras beat it in 2000. No other player has done the Grand Slam in singles and doubles and with the leading players no longer playing doubles; it is a record that won't be broken.

He played with Neale Fraser in seven of his successful doubles campaign, four with Stolle, three with Laver, and one with Ken Fletcher. The only non-Australian was Manolo Santana for the 16th. His only defeats in Grand Slam finals were the three he suffered at the hands of Laver.

John Newcombe

It is difficult to find another era when one country, Australia, was so dominant in men's tennis. There were Ashley Cooper,

Neale Fraser, Fred Stolle, Tony Roche, as well as the players already covered. Another was big-serving John Newcombe, who won 26 Majors in all, albeit 17 in doubles.

He was born in Sydney and loved sport, finally deciding to concentrate on tennis before he was ten. He won junior championships and at nineteen was selected for the Davis Cup in 1964, playing finally in 1973, and captaining the Team between 1994 and 2000.

Partnered by Tony Roche, they won eleven Grand Slam doubles between 1965 and 1971, four each at the Australian and Wimbledon, three French, and one US. He had five different partners in his other doubles successes and two mixed titles at the US and Australian.

His singles Grand Slams were three at Wimbledon and two each in France and the USA, all at that time being played on grass.

FACTS & FIGURES

1. The Open Era of tennis began in 1968 with the first Grand Slam being the French Open at Roland Garros.

2. Wimbledon Tournament is the largest tennis tournament in the world played on grass. It is attended by more than 500,000 people each year.

3. Jean Borotra of France won Wimbledon in 1924, was still playing in the main tournament 40 years later, then in 1977 he played in the Wimbledon veterans' doubles, aged 78.

4. In 1954, Jaroslav Drobný became the only male tennis player to win the Wimbledon singles Championship wearing glasses.

5. For a short time, the French Open, now famous for its Roland Garros clay, was played on grass.

6. In 1953, the French was played on indoor wood at the Palais des Sports.

7. Two-time Grand Slam winner, Ille Nastase, who won the US and French in the early 70s, stood for Mayor of Bucharest in 1996, unsuccessfully.

8. Australian Ashley Cooper's amateur career was brief, but he won eight Grand Slams, including three in 1958, and lost

a five set semi-final in Paris. He turned professional in 1959 at 22 years old.

9. Fred Stolle won nineteen Grand Slams but just two in singles, France 1965 and US 1966. He had lost in five Finals before he eventually won. Four of those defeats were against his regular doubles partner, Roy Emerson.

10. Neale Fraser had two US titles and beat Laver in the Wimbledon final in 1960 but is equally well-known as one of the few players to complete a doubles Grand Slam.

11. Anthony Wilding was engaged to be married to Broadway star Maxine Elliot. She devoted herself after his death to help the World War I effort by organizing and staffing a barge for injured soldiers in France.

12. In 1933, Bunny Austin was the first man to wear shorts at Wimbledon.

13. Left-hander John Doeg prevented Bill Tilden from winning his 8th US Title in 1930 when he served 28 aces in his semi-final win.

14. In any other era, Jacques Brugnon would have been a star of French tennis, but he was slightly overshadowed by the other three French players in the late 20s/early 30s known as the "Four Musketeers". He was a doubles specialist and won ten doubles Grand Slams.

15. Fred Stolle's son, Sandon, played Davis Cup tennis for Australia.

16. Bob Hewitt was a regular double partner of Fred Stolle. He was born in Australia but changed to represent South Africa after marrying a South African lady. He won fifteen Grand Slam doubles titles in the 60s and 70s, often with South African Frew McMillan.

17. Tony Roche won just a single Grand Slam Single title, the French in 1966, though he won fifteen doubles with John Newcombe, his regular Men's doubles partner.

18. Harry Hopman was responsible for a golden era of Australian tennis. He was Davis Cup captain for 22 years and was the man who saw a series of Grand Slam winners emerge from Australia through the period from the mid-50s.

19. One of Hopman's "pupils" was Mal Anderson, who was the first unseeded player to win the US Title in 1957, beating fellow countryman, and No 1 seed, Ashley Cooper

20. Sven Davison was the first Swede to get international prominence at tennis. He won the French singles in 1957.

TRIVIA QUESTIONS

1. What is the famous logo associated with Rene Lacoste?

   A. Elephant

   B. Lion

   C. Crocodile

   D. Tiger

   E. Giraffe

2. Which was the dominant men's tennis nation in the 1960s?

   A. USA

   B. France

   C. Britain

   D. Australia

   E. Spain

3. What nationality were the "Four Musketeers"?

   A. France

   B. Germany

   C. USA

   D. Great Britain

   E. Australia

4. Which player won a calendar Grand Slam twice?

   A. Roy Emerson

B. Ken Rosewall

C. Anthony Wilding

D. Fred Perry

E. Rod Laver

5. Which US Champion joined the Air Force when the US entered the War?

   A. Bill Tilden

   B. Don Budge

   C. Ellsworth Vines

   D. Fred Perry

   E. William Larned

Answers

1. C
2. A
3. D
4. E
5. B

CHAPTER 3

THE OPEN ERA AND THE ATP

Today's stars are truly world figures. The coverage the sport of tennis receives has expanded enormously since the Open Era began. The Tour goes to all parts of the world, and the rewards waiting for the best players were significant in the 1970s, given that before the Open Era they were insignificant. If the 70s was suddenly good, imagine what rewards the 21st Century have brought.

The Grand Slam singles prizes alone are "seven figures", while with nine Masters events and the end of season Championship, a successful season may be even "eight figures."

Here are some of the names that everyone interested in sport will know; they are truly "household names."

Björn Borg

Björn Borg had won a record five successive Wimbledon championships when he suddenly announced his retirement at the tender age of 26. He had been playing senior tennis for over a decade, representing Sweden in the Davis Cup at the age of fifteen and winning both his singles matches. He had been born in Stockholm in 1956 and amassed eleven Grand Slams in all, those five at Wimbledon and six at Roland Garros and the French. Borg was the youngest winner of the French and won Wimbledon in 1976. His final win in 1980 against John McEnroe included a 34-point tie break and is remembered as one of the greatest Wimbledon finals of all time. McEnroe had his revenge in 1981 to end Borg's remarkable run. He retired in January 1983, with 64 titles and a winning singles run of 33 games in the Davis Cup.

He briefly played tennis again and faced some exhibition matches against former rivals, but things were never the same again.

Jimmy Connors

American Jimmy Connors, who won eight Grand Slams and 109 titles in all, was famous for his powerful two-handed backhand. Born in St. Louis in 1952, his mother was a former professional who taught her son to play on a court built in the back garden.

At 16, he trained with Pancho Segura before going to the University of California; he dropped out and opted for professional tennis instead. However, he wouldn't join the ATP and played in independent tournaments. He beat Arthur Ashe in the US Pro singles event in 1973, and then in 1974, he won three Grand Slams in a single season but didn't enter the French. His season record was 99 – 4 and reached No 1. Ranking; he held that for 159 consecutive weeks and for 268 weeks in all.

He won a further four US Opens and the 1982 Wimbledon Title. His last title was in Tel Aviv in 1989, though in 1991 US Open, he beat John McEnroe for two sets down before falling to Jim Courier in the semis. He was 39.

Arthur Ashe

Arthur Ashe from Richmond, Virginia, was the first African American to win the men's singles at Wimbledon and the US Open, as well as being the first African-American man to reach No. 1 in the world. He was born in 1943, and sadly, having been given a blood transfusion of contaminated blood, contracted AIDS and died in 1993 at the age of 49.

He made his first Davis Cup appearance in 1963, and while still an amateur, he won the 1968 US Open. In 1970, he added the Australian Open, but perhaps the most famous victory was when he beat Jimmy Connors at Wimbledon in 1975 when his tactics were to take the pace off the ball. Connors had no answer.

Ashe had health problems; he had a heart attack in 1979 and retired from tennis, but sadly one of the transfusion he received during one of his operations was with infected blood. After retirement, he worked tirelessly for charities and is fondly remembered by everyone, whether they knew him personally or not.

Guillermo Vilas

Guillermo Vilas, the left-handed Argentinian who became known as the "Young Bull of the Pampas", had many talents, including writing songs and screenplays, so touring was never dull.

He won 62 ATP titles including four Grand Slams, the Australian Open in 1978 and 1979, with the French and US Opens coming in 1977. He was a supreme athlete who could wear opponents down. He was especially good on clay as a result.

He was born in Mar de Plata and began professionally in 1970. He lost to Borg in the 1975 French and reached the last four at the US Open in successive years, 1975 and 1976. In 1977, coached by Ion Tiriac, he won seventeen titles and had a singles record 145 – 14.

He played on tour for 19 years, playing his last Grand Slam final in Paris in 1982.

He did win on grass, but not at Wimbledon, while his Davis Cup record was 45 – 10, including 6 – 0 against the USA, including 2 – 0 against McEnroe.

John McEnroe

John McEnroe was born in 1959 in Wiesbaden, West Germany, but the McEnroes returned to New York in 1960. He was a virtual unknown when he reached the semi-finals at Wimbledon as an unseeded 18-year-old with an attitude and plenty of hair with a sweat band around his head. Arguably, his 1980 defeat to Bjorn Borg was the greatest final ever played at Wimbledon. He reversed the result in the final the following year.

After leaving school, he went travelling in Europe, playing a little tennis, and initially was aiming for the Junior Title when he qualified for the Main Draw and reached the last four before losing to Jimmy Connors. He returned to college in the USA but left to play professional tennis. He lost in his next appearance at Wimbledon the following season but reached the fourth round at the US Open. He was picked for the USA Davis Cup team while still in his teens and the USA won for the first time in six years.

His first Grand Slam was the US Open in 1979, and he led the USA in retaining the Davis Cup. That famous final against Borg followed, but McEnroe had revenge in the US Open. After winning Wimbledon in 1981, he had a quiet 1982. He won again in 1983 as well as winning 82 of his 85 matches in 1984, including a third Wimbledon and fourth US Open.

He was still winning in 1985, but no Grand Slams, though he had two doubles successes before retirement, US Open in 1989 and Wimbledon in 1992. Few who listen to his commentary insight into the game today can imagine the rebellious youngster they used to watch, but perhaps he has transferred his rebelliousness elsewhere. Having divorced Tatum O'Neal, he married rock star, Patti Smith.

Ivan Lendl

Ivan Lendl has always said his mission was to win, and he did, taking 100 titles in all. Some see him as impassive and mechanical, others say talented and focused. You have to decide for yourself, but latterly, his approach has certainly helped Andy Murray to his three Grand Slams and two Olympic Golds.

He was born in Ostrava in Czechoslovakia in 1960 and had an extremely productive junior career before playing on the Main Tour. He was world No. 1, winning Junior Wimbledon and the French in 1978. Despite his size, which was ideal for the serve and volley game, he was essentially a baseliner.

While the Wimbledon title eluded Ivan Lendl, he was extremely difficult to beat on any surface other than grass. Born in Czechoslovakia, he later became a US citizen. He won eight Grand Slam titles and appeared in eleven other finals during a career through the 80s and early 90s. He played in at least one final in eleven successive seasons. He was World No. 1 from February 1983 and reinforced that position when beating John McEnroe in the 1985 US Open Final. He held the No. 1 Ranking for 157 weeks. He only lost that ranking briefly in the next five years and had 270 weeks at the top in all.

Boris Becker

Boris Becker burst on to the scene in 1985 by winning the Wimbledon title at the tender age of 17, the youngest player at the time to win a title of that magnitude. He won five more Grand Slams and 49 titles before he retired.

He was born in Leimen in West Germany in 1967 and took to tennis immediately. He actually turned professional at 16. He won Wimbledon and regained the title in 1987 before losing to Stefan Edberg a year later. He won again in 1989, adding the US Open for the first time that autumn. He took the Australian Open in 1991 to become World No. 1 for the first time with his final Grand Slam in 1996, the Australian Open again.

He led Germany to the Davis Cup in 1988 and 1989, winning twenty-two consecutive singles matches at one point. He and Michael Stich won Olympic gold in the doubles in 1992, while among his other successes there were three ATP World Championships. He retired after a fourth round defeat at Wimbledon in 1999.

His involvement in tennis has continued with work both for the media as well as acting as coach/mentor for Novak Djokovic for a time.

Stefan Edberg

Sweden's Stefan Edberg was born in Vastervik in Sweden in 1966 and went on to win six Grand Slam singles titles, as well as three doubles. He won four Junior Grand Slam events in 1983 before turning professional later in the year and winning a doubles event shortly afterwards.

He won his first singles in 1984 in Milan and the Olympic exhibition event. He reached the US Open doubles final with Anders Jarryd later in the year. In those days, the Australian Open was played on grass, so those two, in 1985 and 1987, and his Wimbledon titles, 1988 and 1990, proved his quality on grass. He was a serve and volley player but in fact was comfortable on any surface, though the faster the better. For example, he never won the singles at Roland Garros on the clay. He won 41 singles and 18 doubles titles in his career, and 801 singles matches.

Andre Agassi

Andre Agassi was born in 1970 and became one of the most colourful personalities on the ATP circuit throughout the 1990s. He turned professional at sixteen, winning his first Grand Slam at Wimbledon in 1992. Within three years, he had won the US Open in 1994, and the Australian in 1995. His ranking dropped remarkably after that, but he regained his form to win a very popular French Open in 1999 and the US Open again later in the year.

His father was of Iranian descent, an Olympic boxer, and he encouraged and coached his son from an early age. He trained full-time from his mid-teens and moved from his home in Las Vegas to Florida and the Nick Bollettieri Tennis Academy where many famous players have been coached over the years.

He turned professional in 1986, and his long hair and colourful clothing were a sponsor's dream. After his Australian Open, the next major success was Gold in the 1996 Olympics prior to his slump.

He had three more Grand Slams in the 21st Century, winning the Australian Open in 2000, 2001, and 2003 before retiring in 2006. The world waits with anticipation to see whether his children with his wife, Steffi Graf, have any interest in and any ability at tennis.

Pete Sampras

Pete Sampras, from Maryland, USA, was born of Greek parents in 1971. He went on to win fourteen Grand Slam titles, a record at that time, including seven Wimbledon titles, also a record until beaten by Roger Federer in 2017. He also won five US Open titles and was thus the dominant force in men's tennis through the 1990s.

He turned professional at sixteen and looked a great prospect from an early age.

In 1990, as a 19-year-old, he beat Agassi in straight sets for his first US Open title, having also beaten McEnroe and Lendl en route to the final. He won Wimbledon for the first time in 1993 and took his first Australian title the following January. He dominated Wimbledon with four successive wins between 1997 and 2000.

He passed Roy Emerson's Grand Slam record when winning in 2000, but he wasn't finished. In 2002, he won his 14th and last Grand Slam at the US Open at the age of 31 before retiring a year later.

Jim Courier

Jim Courier was born in 1970 in Florida and proved to be a difficult player to break down because of his strong baseline play. He won four Grand Slams, and although he did not win them all, he was the youngest player to reach the final of the four at just under 23. He was World No. 1 in 1992 and had a career with twenty-three singles titles and six doubles titles. His first Grand Slam was the 1991 French Open where he beat Andre Agassi, a fellow pupil of Nick Bollettieri, in five sets and he won again in 1992.

He had started professionally in 1989 with a five set win over Stefan Edberg in Basel and lost to him in straight sets in the US Open later, in 1991, after his success at Roland Garros.

He was to win in Australia in 1992 and 1993; all four of his Grand Slams between 1991 and 1993. During that spell, he was World No. 1 for 58 weeks. He was famous for his baseball cap and strong double-handed backhand. He played in seven Davis Cups for the USA, winning twice and captaining the side in 2011.

Roger Federer

Roger Federer's 20th Grand Slam title in the Australian Open has reinforced claims that he is the best male tennis player ever, and some would even say the greatest sportsman ever. He was born in Switzerland in 1981 and immediately showed huge promise. He turned professional at seventeen, and his defeat of current champion Pete Sampras at Wimbledon in 2001 announced his arrival to the world.

He has made Wimbledon his "home" with eight Championships between 2003 and 2017. He began 2004 as World No. 2 and won three of the four Grand Slams to start 2005 as No. 1. He won his third successive Wimbledon and another US Open.

He was No. 1 through to 2008, regularly winning Grand Slams, but with the presence of Rafael Nadal was unable to win at Roland Garros in the French Open. That changed in 2009 when Robin Soderling caused a major upset, defeating Nadal. Federer beat Soderling in the final.

It was at Wimbledon that season that he won his 15th Grand Slam to pass Pete Sampras' existing record. He won Wimbledon twice more in 2012 and 2014, but then the Grand Slams dried up at seventeen, until Australia in 2016 when he defeated Nadal in five sets, and Wimbledon followed for a record eight titles. The recent 20th is a real milestone. He has 97 singles titles to date and has spent 302 weeks as World No. 1 over the years. He may return there in the coming months depending upon the schedule he decides upon. Switzerland won the Davis Cup in 2014, and he won Olympic Gold in the doubles in 2008 and silver in the singles in 2012.

Rafael Nadal

Rafael Nadal can rightly claim to be the best clay court tennis player ever. His win in 2017 was his 10th in the French Open and his 16th Grand Slam Title. He was born in 1986 and turned professional at fifteen. He started young, three years old, with uncle Toni who decided to get him to play left-handed. He reached the Wimbledon third round at seventeen, and at nineteen took the French Open, one of eleven titles, eight on clay, in 2005 and No. 3 World Ranking. He won the French Open for the next four years and beat Roger Federer in the Wimbledon final as well as taking Olympic singles Gold. He won the Australian in 2009, but then surprisingly lost in Paris, one of only two times he has done so to date.

He completed his Grand Slam by winning the US Open in 2010, already being holder of the French and Wimbledon.

Novak Djokovic was now serious competition to Nadal and Federer, with Nadal having periods out of the game often due to knee problems. His domination of the French Open continued, though Djokovic beat him in the 2015 tournament. After losing to Federer in Australia in 2017, he took the French Title again, and later in the year the US Open. All the Grand Slams in 2017 therefore went to the "veterans."

Nadal has won the Davis Cup with Spain, Olympic Gold in the 2016 doubles event, and has regained the World No. 1 Ranking. He currently has seventy-five singles titles.

Novak Djokovic

Serbian Novak Djokovic was born in Belgrade in 1987 and is one of four tennis players that have dominated the game in recent years, the others being Federer, Nadal, and Andy Murray. Djokovic has had a significant amount of time as World No. 1, and his twelve Grand Slams include at least one of each of the four Championships.

He was identified as promising when he was very young and began to be trained from the age of six. At thirteen, he went to Munich for more advanced work. At fourteen, he was European champion for his age, and by sixteen, he won a competition in Budapest having come through the qualifiers.

He won the Australian Open in 2008, a tournament in which he has an excellent record. Two years later, Serbia won the Davis Cup, and Djokovic took three of the four Grand Slams and No. 1 Ranking. It took him until 2016 before he could add the French Open to his CV so that he held all four titles at the same time. He could not win another Grand Slam that season however.

He has suffered periods of injury subsequently, but he returned to play at the 2018 Australian Open, so the " battle " of the top four may be joined again soon, and he may be able to add to this 68 singles titles.

Andy Murray

Andy Murray become the first British male in 77 years to win Wimbledon when he beat Novak Djokovic in 2013. Born in Dunblane, Scotland, in 1987, he turned professional in 2005, having already shown his promise at junior level, winning the Junior US Open and being ranked World No. 1.

He beat Federer soon after turning professional but was to lose to him in his first Grand Slam final, the US Open in 2008. He reached World No. 2 in 2009, but Grand Slams eluded him; he lost successive Australian Opens in 2010 and 2011 and then the Wimbledon final in 2012.

He won Olympic Gold in London in 2012, getting revenge over Federer, and was to retain that Title in Rio four years later. His first Grand Slam was the US Open a few weeks after the Olympics with that Wimbledon Title following the next season. In 2016, he won his second Wimbledon.

His appearances in the later stages of Grand Slams confirm his quality, though he has suffered his share of injuries as well. He lost in the Australian final for the 5th time in 2016, and then made his only appearance in the French final, again losing to Djokovic in 2016. He was World No. 1 later in the year until Rafael Nadal took over in 2017.

Murray also led Britain to Davis Cup success in 2016 where his strength in the two singles he played each tie pivotal in the success.

FACTS & FIGURES

1. The longest tennis match in history was the first round match between American John Isner and Frenchman Nicolas Mahut at Wimbledon over three days in 2010. It took 11 hours and 5 minutes over three days, being suspended because of light two nights in a row. Isner finally won 6-4, 3-6, 6-7 (7), 7-6 (3), 70-68. Not surprisingly Isner lost in the next round.

2. The fifth set remains the longest set in history in terms of time and games played; 8 hours 11 minutes and 138 games.

3. The fastest serve recorded at the Australian Open 2006 was Taylor Dent at 231km/hr.

4. In 1985, Boris Becker was the first unseeded player to win Wimbledon.

5. In 2013, the Wimbledon total prize money was the highest of four grand slam tournaments at $34m followed by the US Open at $32m, the Australian Open at $30m, and the French Open at $29m.

6. The 1970 US Open was the first of the Grand Slam to use the tie-break. The US Open is still the only one of the four

to have final set tiebreaks so that record of Isner and Mahut will not be broken in the USA.

7. The longest match in US Open was in 1992, when the men's singles semi-final between Stefan Edberg and Michael Chang took 5 hours and 26 minutes.

8. In 2005, all US Open tennis courts had blue inner courts and green outer courts to improve vision.

9. A year later, the US Open was the first Grand Slam tournament to use Hawk-Eye to review umpire calls.

10. Andy Murray was an 8-year-old schoolboy when a gunman broke into his Dunblane school, killing many pupils and a teacher before shooting himself.

11. Roger Federer is the father of two sets of twins, the first girls and the second boys. He travels everywhere with the family.

12. Rafael Nadal appeared in a hit video by Shakira, "I'm a Gypsy", despite being a Real Madrid fan and Shakira's husband being a star with Barcelona, Gerald Pique.

13. Jimmy Connors was once engaged to fellow tennis star Chris Evert, but they broke up while both of them were riding high in the World Rankings.

14. Novak Djokovic is fluent in English, German, and Italian, as well as his native Serbian.

15. Boris Becker's competitive instincts these days are satisfied at the poker table, though it is a game where he must hide his feelings a little better than he did at times on the tennis court.

16. Andre Agassi and his wife Steffi Graf have a huge number of Grand Slams between them; Agassi has eight and his wife a huge twenty-two.

17. John McEnroe helped the USA win five Davis Cups and showed his commitment to the Competition by also taking the role of non-playing captain.

18. Pete Sampras has thalassemia minor, a condition that many people of Mediterranean descent suffer from. He causes him to tire more quickly than others when they are doing any form of strenuous exercise.

19. Arthur Ashe has a Courage Reward in his name for people who go that little bit further than would be expected. Nelson Mandela and Muhammad Ali are past winners, but some are just fairly anonymous, ordinary people who show real bravery.

20. Guillermo Vilas never had the honour of being World No. 1. In 2015, Argentine journalist Eduardo Puppo feels that an error was made in 1975 and asked for the ATP to look at the evidence and rule retrospectively. Unfortunately for Vilas, the ATP has declined to do so, feeling it could set a precedent.

TRIVIA QUESTIONS

1. How many points were played in the famous tie-break between Borg and McEnroe in 1980?

    A. 24
    B. 27
    C. 30
    D. 32
    E. 34

2. Whose record number of Grand Slam wins did Federer beat to become the first player to fifteen titles?

    A. Rafael Nadal
    B. Pete Sampras
    C. Bjorn Borg
    D. Stefan Edberg
    E. Jimmy Connors

3. What record does Rafael Nadal hold in Grand Slams?

    A. He was the youngest ever winner of a Grand Slam
    B. He was the first left-hander to win a Grand Slam
    C. He has the most Grand Slam titles
    D. He has won 10 times at one of the Grand Slams
    E. He has never lost in a Grand Slam final

4. Pete Sampras was how old when he won his first Grand Slam?

   A. 17
   B. 18
   C. 19
   D. 20
   E. 21

5. When did Novak Djokovic win the last of the four Grand Slams to complete the full set?

   A. 2016
   B. 2015
   C. 2014
   D. 2013
   E. 2012

Answers

1. E
2. B
3. D
4. C
5. A

CHAPTER 4
WOMEN BEFORE THE WTA

The early game of tennis was so much different than what today's audience watch. That is not so much about athleticism as dress. Women entered the court and played the game in what would be regarded as almost formal dress. Today's players would probably say it was impossible to run in long dresses and white long-sleeved blouses. The women tennis players used to do that, though they rarely covered the court as women do today.

Tennis was not a game that working class girls played in the days as the game developed. However, the names that won championships are just as important to the history of the game as everyone else. Champions had things easier in the early days because all the other entrants to a competition had to play for the right to meet the defending champion so it was easier for women, and men for that matter, to put a run of wins together.

Here are some of the names that you may not be familiar with and some you surely will know.

Blanche Bingley Hillyard

Great Britain's Blanche Bingley Hillyard holds the record for the most Wimbledon singles final appearance, thirteen between her first in 1886 and her last in 1900. She first played there as a 20-year-old in 1884 and won in 1886, and in 1900, she established the record for being the oldest champion at 37 years of age, though the record was not to last. Her rival Lottie Dod defeated her five times in the final, but she was more than happy with her four titles. Her last Wimbledon was in 1913, aged 48.

In those days, there was little international travel though Hillyard did win the German Championships twice and the Irish three times. The South of England Championships at Eastbourne was thought of as a major championship and she won there eleven times between 1885 and 1905.

Lottie Dod

Dod came from a small village close to Liverpool, some distance away from the All England Club in terms of travelling when she first appeared at Wimbledon in 1887. There was a concession on what she could wear because of being just fifteen; it was a bit like a school uniform, black stockings and shoes, a white cap, and calf-length dress. It gave her an advantage over the women in full-length dresses, and she made it count.

She became the youngest champion in the history of Wimbledon. Her ground strokes were hard, and she would volley and smash, a style not yet adopted by others. Her opponent in 1887 was the defending champion, Blanche Bingley Hillyard, whom she beat 6-2, 6-0, winning the ten straight games from 2 – 2 in the first set. The second set lasted just ten minutes. She was to beat Hillyard in four more finals, 1888 and then three years in a row, 1891 – 93.

She gave up tennis to play golf and was British Champion in 1904 while she was in the 1908 Olympic Archery team that won the Silver Medal.

Dorothea Lambert Chambers

Dorothea showed no mercy on court, and two of her seven Wimbledon Titles saw her have extremely easy wins. In 1911, he didn't lose a single game to Dora Boothby, who herself had been champion two years earlier. In 1904, her second win, she lost just three games. Other than her first title, 1903, all her wins were in straight sets, though it has to be said that she lost five finals as well.

Her Wimbledon career spanned nearly two decades; she was a losing finalist in 1919 and 1920, both times to Suzanne Lenglen. She was the oldest finalist at 41 years of age. She was four years older when she played her last Wightman Cup, and her singles win was decisive in a 4 – 4 GB victory.

In 1908, she won the outdoor Gold Medal in the Olympics.

She appeared in three doubles and a single mixed final without success in the later stages of her career and ironically was beaten 6 – 0, 6 – 0 in the mixed final of 1919.

Suzanne Lenglen

Suzanne Lenglen was born in 1899, in Compiegne, and was the dominant force in women's tennis until the mid-1920s when she turned professional. The French Open Trophy bears her name in tribute to the contribution she made to French tennis; indeed, tennis everywhere.

She began with a cheap racquet, but quickly her father saw she was serious about the game so bought an expensive one and a backboard to practise against. She joined the exclusive Nice Club at eleven, and she followed a strenuous regime.

Lenglen began winning regional championships in 1912, and a year later won the Nice Tennis Club championship, followed by the Italian championship in 1914. Stories of her prowess were spreading. She won the World Hard Court Championships in singles and doubles soon afterwards, but the War then intervened. She continued to play where possible, often against men at the Nice Club.

In 1919, she headed for Wimbledon and won, including an epic against Lambert Chambers, a seven-time Wimbledon Champion. Despite her continued success, she lacked confidence and was often ill or depressed. Her only defeats seemed to be defaults.

She turned professional, but the circuit was a failure and she was not allowed to regain her amateur status. Throughout the 30s, her health remained poor, and in 1938 she died of pernicious anaemia.

Helen Wills Moody

Helen Wills won 180 straight matches from 1927 to 1933 without losing a single set. Her career record was nineteen Major singles titles, and fourteen of them were during that winning streak. In addition, she took nine doubles and three mixed titles.

She was not popular with the media, who dubbed her "Little Miss Poker Face." "I'll let my racquet do the talking" was her attitude. She was slight at 5 feet high but hit with power that meant other aspects of her game hardly mattered.

"She hit the ball harder than most, except maybe Steffi Graf," said Don Budge. "Her footwork didn't have to be great. She would control the play because she hit the ball so hard."

She was the daughter of a surgeon so had a privileged upbringing. She got a racquet at fourteen with membership of the Berkeley Tennis Club in California. She learned by watching others and at seventeen won the first of her US Titles. Her eight Wimbledon Titles came from nine appearances, with the last in 1938.

Her best season was 1928, with three Grand Slam singles. She won Gold in singles and doubles in the 1928 Olympics and played Wightman Cup between 1923 and 1938. She still enjoyed a game into her 80s.

Helen Hull Jacobs

Jacobs and Helen Wills Moody was a rivalry that went down in history.

It dominated women's tennis in the 1930s with Moody beating her in four Wimbledon finals as well as at the US and the French. Aside from that, Jacobs still won five Grand Slam singles, three doubles, and a mixed, as well as reaching eighteen finals.

Her only win against Moody was in the 1933 US when Moody retired with a bad back when trailing 3 – 0 in the deciding set. Jacobs was named Female Athlete of the Year in 1933 by the Associated Press. Three years later, she was on the cover of Times Magazine in a proposed new style of clothing for women's tennis; black shirt with white trim and tailored shorts. At the time, she had won four straight US titles but she failed to get a fifth, beaten by Alice Marble.

She won the Wimbledon Title just once, in 1936, in three sets against Hilde Krahwinkel.

Jacobs won the US doubles in 1932,1934, and 1935 as well as the mixed in 1934, and representing USA in the Wightman Cup, she was on the winning side ten times out of twelve. She finally retired in 1947.

Louise Brough Clapp

Althea Louise Brough was born in Oklahoma City before the family moved to Beverley Hills, California, and she learnt her tennis on the public courts as a teenager before going to the University of Southern California. She went on to win 35 Grand Slam titles. She won three national juniors before entering university and also played in the US National itself.

She won Wimbledon four times, three in a row between 1948 and 1950, as well as the Australian and the US. Her total of twenty-one women's doubles Grand Slams is unlikely ever to be beaten, while she also won eight mixed. Twelve of those doubles were the US, playing with Margaret Osborne duPont, with successive wins between 1942 and 1950.

She went just once to Australia and brought back the singles and doubles. In the ten years she played at Wimbledon, she appeared in twenty-one of the thirty finals played.

She won all three events three times, in the 1947 US, at Wimbledon a year later, and again in 1950. Her serve and volley style was ideally suited to grass, and thirty of those thirty-five successes were on that surface.

In the Wightman Cup, she was undefeated in twenty-two matches.

Margaret Osborne duPont

Margaret Osborne duPont was born on a ranch in Oregon before the family moved to Spokane in Washington and then San Francisco where she learnt her tennis on the public courts. She had success as a junior before playing in the main competitions.

She won thirty-seven Grand Slam Titles in a long and successful career with thirty-one coming in doubles and mixed doubles. She was most impressive in her home tournament, winning twenty-five at the US Nationals, including thirteen in the doubles, twelve with Louise Brough (ten in a row) with whom she won eight more elsewhere. She spent an impressive two decades ranked in the World's top ten.

She was 44 when she won the mixed title with Neale Fraser in 1962. Her six singles Championships had been the French in 1946 and 1948; Wimbledon in 1947 and US Nationals three year in a row, 1948-50. Her 1948 win over Brough had been a marathon; 4-6, 6-4, 15-13. Brough beat her in three of her four other singles finals appearances.

She never went down to Australian to play as her husband, who had some health problems, preferred California at that time of year.

DuPont played in the Wightman Cup team every year from 1946 to 1958, winning all her games, ten singles and nine doubles.

Pauline Betz

In 1947, Pauline Betz Addie was banned from the major tournaments for deciding to pursue a professional career. At that time, she was on a run of thirty-nine successive wins. She had won the US Nationals four times already and the Wimbledon Title to go with one of those US Titles in 1946. She was ranked World No. 1 but was banned just because of inferring she would turn professional; she had not signed a contract.

She had no choice than to play professionally which she did for thirteen more seasons.

Betz was born in Dayton, Ohio, and learnt the game on the public courts in Los Angeles where her mother was a PE teacher in Watts. She was given a scholarship to Rollins College in Florida and played No. 4 in the Men's team.

From 1941 until 1946, she appeared in each of the finals in the US Nationals, beating Louise Brough in 1942 and 1943, and also beating her doubles partner, Doris Hart in the 1946 final. Their record as a doubles partnership was excellent, though they never actually managed to win a title from several final appearances.

Her mixed title was the French in 1946, playing with Budge Patty.

Mo Connelly

"Little Mo" achieved the calendar Grand Slam at the age of eighteen in 1953, the first to do so, and by a margin the youngest. Her career only lasted four years, but in that time, she won nine Grand Slam singles, two doubles, and a single mixed. Her leg was crushed when she was horse riding and was hit by a car. In 1969, at the very young age of 34, Connolly died from cancer which had been diagnosed three years earlier.

She was just 5 feet 4 inches and hailed from San Diego, California. She was coached from the age of ten and won the National Junior Indoor title four years later. Her first US Championship was at just under seventeen in 1951, and she repeated that in the following two seasons.

She had three Wimbledon wins, two in Paris, and one in Australia. She won in all her nine finals, and her overall Grand Slam record was 53 – 2. She played Wightman Cup, of course, four wins from four.

Doris Hart

Doris Hart was the first player to win a career Grand Slam in all events, something only Margaret Court and Martina Navratilova have matched in women's tennis. Only twice in thirty-four Grand Slam singles events did she fail to reach the quarter-finals, reaching eighteen finals and winning six titles.

Her best day was in 1951, when she won the three Wimbledon titles on the same day after rain upset the scheduling. Her Grand Slam record included fourteen doubles and fifteen mixed, from thirty and eighteen final appearances respectively. In 1954, she won all three in both the French and US Championships.

Hart came from St. Louis but grew up in Coral Gables, Florida, and after winning the US Girls' singles championship in 1942 and 1943 and doubles titles in 1940 and 1943, she went to the University of Miami from 1947 until 1949. She began to play in major tournaments at just fifteen and ultimately won 325 titles. Her Wightman Cup record was 14 – 0 in singles and 8 – 1 in doubles.

Althea Gibson

Althea Gibson was born in the small town of Silver, South Carolina, but the family moved to Harlem in 1930. On August 25, 1950, she became the first African-American to play in the US National Championships. It was an enormous step for African-Americans, and happily she beat Barbara Knapp 6 – 2, 6 – 2 that day. She lost 9 – 7 in the third set in the next round to Louise Brough Clapp, having led 7 – 6 before a rain interruption.

It was a few years before she won any of her major titles. Between 1956 and 1958, she reached nineteen major finals and won eleven times.

Gibson began in the American Tennis Association (ATA), the oldest African-American sports organization in the USA, the black equivalent to the United States Lawn Tennis Association and founded in 1916. She won the Junior National Championships at seventeen and eighteen years old, and from 1947 won ten straight ATA National titles. Pressure was exerted as she emerged so that she was finally allowed that appearance in August 1950, and the international story began from there.

She won the French in 1956, then for the next two years won both Wimbledon and the US. During that time, she won the doubles in France and Wimbledon in 1956, the Australian and Wimbledon in 1957, as well as the US mixed, and won the Wimbledon doubles again in 1958.

She turned professional and competed on the US circuit in 1960, but there was limited prize money, so she switched to golf, joining the LPGA Tour in 1964 at the age of 37.

Maria Bueno

Brazil issued a postage stamp to honour Maria Bueno and her 1959 and 1960 Wimbledon Ladies singles championship titles. In all, she won nineteen of thirty-five major singles, doubles, and mixed doubles opportunities. Up to this time, the only women to have won both Wimbledon and the US in the same year, 1959, had been American.

She was ranked No. 1 in the world in 1959, 1960, 1964, and 1966, and won both Wimbledon and the US titles three times. In addition, she won doubles and mixed, sixteen in all with six different partners.

She came from Sao Paulo and won each of the age group National Championship as she grew up and first played on the Caribbean circuit before heading to Europe. Her first Wimbledon Title was at the age of seventeen in 1959 and retained the title the following year. She couldn't retain the US she won in 1959 but had three more titles, 1963, 1964, and 1966.

Five of her eleven doubles wins were with Darlene Hard and her sole mixed title was with Don Howe in the 1960 French, the same year that she won her only Australian Title playing with Christine Truman.

Bueno's career effectively ended before the Open Era, though in 1974 he earned money winning the Japanese Open to add to her sixty-two wins as an amateur.

Margaret Court

Between 1960 and 1975, Margaret Court (nee Smith) won twenty-four Grand Slam singles championships, as well as twenty-one mixed, including two calendar Grand Slams, and nineteen doubles. In 1970, she matched Mo Connolly's record of a calendar Grand Slam. In three other years, 1965, 1969, and 1973, she had three wins. Her overall career record was 1,180-107 which is a stunning percentage.

Margaret Smith was born in Albury, New South Wales, Australia, and won the first of her seven successive Australian singles in

1960 at seventeen. She finished with eleven in all. She had three children, returning to tennis after each, though after the birth of her third in 1975, she was close to the end of her career.

Her only final defeat was in 1971 at Wimbledon when she was beaten by Evonne Goolagong. Her toughest win was probably the 3rd leg of her 1970 Grand Slam when she beat Billie Jean King 14 – 12, 11 – 9 in the days before tie breaks.

Australia won four Federations Cups with Court in the side between 1964 and 1970.

Billie Jean King

Few tennis players, on or off the court, have had the historical impact of Billie Jean, an activist of whom CNN in 2015, under the title "Leading Women," talked of "extraordinary women of our time, remarkable professionals who have made it to the top in all areas of business, the arts, sport, culture, science, and more." King was included in a list of seven with author and anti-slavery campaigner Harriet Beecher Stowe, writer of Holocaust diary Anne Frank, and Rosalind Franklin, the scientist that helped the world to understand DNA.

Her Grand Slam record reads thirty-nine over the three competitions, including twelve singles, eight in the Open Era. Her first Grand Slam was an amateur, Wimbledon 1966. It took her until 1972 to achieve the career Grand Slam when she beat Evonne Goolagong at the French. She had achieved that in the mixed category four years earlier.

King was born Billie Jean Moffitt and grew up in Long Beach, California, within a sporting family; brother Randy had an eleven year professional baseball career. She won her last title just short of her 40th birthday and was the first woman to pass $100,000 prize money in a calendar year.

She helped form the Women's Tennis Association and fought tirelessly to achieve equal prize money for women. In 2009, she was awarded the Presidential Medal of Freedom by President Barack Obama, the first female "athlete" to receive the US highest peacetime honour.

FACTS & FIGURES

1. The longest women's tennis match was in 1984 between Vicki Nelson and Jean Hepner at the 'Ginny of Richmond' in Richmond, Virginia. It lasted 6 hours, 31 minutes; the score of 6–4, 7–6, including a 29-minute, 643-shot rally.

2. The shortest recorded tennis match lasted just 20 minutes, Susan M. Tutt beating Marion Bandy 6-0, 6-0 at the Wimbledon in 1969.

3. The first overseas winner at Wimbledon was May Sutton of the USA who was the ladies' champion in 1905. Australian Norman Brookes was the first foreign Men's Champion, in 1907.

4. Before 1946, women played in full length dresses and men played in full length trousers. It couldn't have been easy to play, particularly a long game on a hot day.

5. Billie Jean King received a £25 gift voucher for winning Wimbledon; compare that to today, but the amateur regulations were strict and always enforced.

6. Rosie Casals won seven Grand Slam doubles and was runner up seven times between 1966 and 1975 playing

7. with Billie Jean King; in all she won 112 doubles titles, half with King.

8. Florence Angela Margaret Mortimer Barrett won an all-English final at Wimbledon in 1961 beating Christine Truman Janes.

9. Anne Hayden Jones was the first left-hander to win the Wimbledon singles when she beat Billie Jean King in 1969. She had previously won the French and the US twice each.

10. There was almost a decade between Virginia Wade's first Grand Slam, the US in 1968 beating King, and 1977 winning Wimbledon against Betty Stove. In between, she won in Australia in 1972.

11. In 2018, at the Australian Open Billie Jean King called on Australian tennis to take Margaret Court's name off the arena because of her views on gay rights.

12. Charlotte Cooper became the oldest female player at just short of thirty-eight to win Wimbledon when she won the 1908 title against Agnes Morton, 6-4, 6-4.

13. Helen Hull Jacobs was a US naval intelligence commander during the War.

14. The first of Margaret duPont's thirteen US doubles titles was with Sarah Palfrey in 1941.

15. Margaret DuPont and Louise Brough won twelve of the fourteen US championships in which they played and 58 of 60 matches.

16. Pauline Betz played No. 4 on the men's team of Rollins College when Jack Kramer was the No.1.

17. Sarah Palfrey Danzig Cooke won eleven Grand Slam doubles in the 1930s and 40s with five different partners before being banned by the US in 1947 for deciding to turn professional.

18. She won the US Clay Court mixed in 1945, playing with her husband. They had played together in the Cincinnati years before in the Men's doubles when there was a shortage of men.

19. Between 1936 and 1940, American Alice Marble won her National Championship four times and Wimbledon one.

20. Bobby Riggs partnered with Marble to the Wimbledon mixed when she won all three titles; her Women's doubles partner was Sarah Palfrey.

21. Margaret Court is now a preacher, at one time travelling around Australia.

TRIVIA QUESTIONS

1. Who was dubbed "Little Miss Poker Face"?

   A. Mo Connolly

   B. Helen Wills Moody

   C. Maria Bueno

   D. Margaret Court

   E. Billie Jean King

2. Who was the only player to beat Margaret Court in a Grand Slam final?

   A. Evonne Goolagong

   B. Billie Jean King

   C. Maria Bueno

   D. Christine Truman

   E. Virginia Wade

3. Name the US Woman with a 14 – 0 Wightman Cup singles record.

   A. Rosie Casals

   B. Billie Jean King

   C. Helen Wills Moody

   D. Mo Connolly

   E. Doris Hart

4. Who was banned from amateur competition simply by hinting she would turn professional?

    A. Louise Brough Clapp
    B. Althea Gibson
    C. Margaret Osbourne duPont
    D. Pauline Betz
    E. Helen Hull Jacobs

5. What was historical about Althea Gibson's appearance at the US Nationals in 1950?

    A. She was the first left hander to play in the singles.
    B. She was reinstated as an amateur after playing professionally.
    C. She was the first African to play there.
    D. She had to borrow kit to play as hers was lost in transit.
    E. She was the first player of African-American descent to play.

Answers

1. B
2. A
3. C
4. D
5. E

CHAPTER 5
THE OPEN ERA AND THE WTA

The riches available to the top women tennis players contrasts starkly with what was available when the Open Era started. It is not just the prize money but also the endorsements and sponsorship opportunities that have continued to increase by the decade. In the coming years, there are huge opportunities for the next generation of "champions" as Serena Williams approaches the end of her career. At present, no other woman tennis player can firmly state her case as the world's best. There are interesting times ahead.

Evonne Goolagong

Evonne Goolagong was one of eight children born in the wheat town of Barrellan in New South Wales. Home was a tin shack without electricity. Of Aborigine heritage, she faced prejudice and an uncertain future.

Her first racquet was made from a fruit box and looked like a paddle; it had no strings. The local club president asked if she wanted to join, as she regularly peered through the fence. Bill Kurtzman can rightly feel proud of that gesture in an environment that was still very difficult for Aborigines. She showed promise, which led to coach Vic Edwards travelling from Sydney to see her. He persuaded Evonne's parents to let her school in Sydney and develop her talents. At fifteen, she was New South Wales Champion and soon competed in the Nationals.

Goolagong appeared in twenty-six major finals (18 singles, six women's doubles and two mixed), winning seven singles, five doubles and one mixed championship. Overall on tour, she won seventy-two singles, forty-five doubles and three mixed doubles.

In the 1971 Australian Open, Goolagong lost to her idol Margaret Court in three sets, 2-6, 7-6, 7-5 but then won her first major singles championship in Paris weeks later and followed that up by beating Court at Wimbledon. Her 1980 success was against another legend, Chris Evert. Her Australian wins included three in a row, 1974 – 6, and four in all. She lost in four US finals so was unable to do the Grand Slam of Titles.

She retired in 1983 after a series of nagging injuries but she had certainly made her mark.

Chris Evert

Chris Evert was born in Florida in 1954, and after a career spanning a decade and a half, she retired in 1989 with eighteen Grand Slam singles titles and a record for career winning percentage. Her first Grand Slam was the French in 1974, but she first hit the headlines as a 15-year-old when she beat

Margaret Court in North Carolina. She reached the semi-finals of the US Open in 1971 and went on to reach at least that stage for the next thirty-three as well.

In 1974, she won fifty-five singles in a row, including the French and Wimbledon, retaining the French and getting the US Title in 1975. He had to wait until 1982 to complete her Grand Slam when she won in Australia. Her most successful event was the French where she won seven times.

She vied with Navratilova throughout her career and the two had many famous battles as well as playing some doubles together.

Martina Navratilova

Czech tennis star Martina Navratilova emerged to challenge Evert with their having many famous games. She was born in 1956 in Prague, and after her mother remarried, she took her stepfather's name. He became her first coach, and tennis was in her blood; her grandmother had been a very good player.

She became national champion at fifteen and turned professional a year later. Realising the problems of living under Russian control, she defected at eighteen at the 1975 US Open and was therefore cut off from her family for a long time.

Her first Grand Slam was Wimbledon in 1978, and she retained the title, adding the Australian in 1981. She lost just six matches in three years between 1982 and 1984. Her eighteen Grand

Slam singles titles in which she won nine at Wimbledon from twelve finals. In addition, she won thirty-one doubles and ten mixed. While she retired from singles in 1994, she continued to play doubles. She won the mixed at Wimbledon in 2003 and the doubles in the US in 2006.

Tracy Austin

Tracey Austin set a record when she won a professional tournament in 1977 at fourteen years of age, and she looked it with pigtails and braces. It is to her credit that in the era of Evert and Navratilova, she briefly got to No. 1 in the World Rankings. She was just sixteen when she beat Evert in the US Open final to stop Evert making it five wins on the trot. Years earlier, she had ended Evert's 125 match clay court winning streak at the 1979 Italian Open.

She won the US Open again two years later in 1981, this time beating Navratilova but her career was brief. Injury forced her to retire in 1983, but she still managed twenty-nine singles titles. One of her proudest days was winning Wimbledon mixed in 1980 with brother John.

She wasn't completely finished and has remained involved in tennis. She won the 2005 doubles at Wimbledon with Jana Novotna.

Steffi Graf

Steffi Graf was born in 1969, in Mannheim, West Germany, and turned professional at just thirteen. By the time she retired in 1999, she had won twenty-two Grand Slam singles, including a 1988 Grand Slam together with Olympic gold. Both her parents had been tennis players, so her interest was natural. She actually won a junior competition when only six.

Tennis was just a demonstration event in 1984, and she took the honorary gold. Her first Grand Slam title was the French Open in 1987, defeating Martina Navratilova, and by the summer, she was World No. 1 where she stayed for 186 consecutive weeks.

In October 1991, she reached 500 career wins and continued to collect Grand Slams throughout the 90s although injuries became more common late in the decade. When she finally retired, she had won over $21m and won each of the Grand Slams at least four times. She won the French in 1999 then lost a close final at Wimbledon. A few weeks' later, she retired.

Arantxa Sánchez Vicario

Arantxa was born in Barcelona in 1970 and started tennis when she was just four years old and had the advantage of two brothers who became professionals. She was small but powerful and the French was certainly her favourite venue; she won the singles there three times, 1989, 1994, and 1998. She also became the first Spaniard to win the US Open in 1994 when she defeated Steffi Graf.

The following two seasons, she reached the Wimbledon final, only to lose. She also never won in the Australian but did reach the final. She actually reached World No. 1 briefly in 1995.

She won six doubles in Grand Slams as well as four mixed. Jana Novotna was her partner for three of her doubles, US (1994), and the Australian and Wimbledon (1995) in that order. She had previously won the Australian in 1993 with Helena Sukova and won the US later in the season. Her 6th Title was Australia in 1996. Her mixed titles were the French twice, Australian, and US between 1992 to 2000.

She played in the Federations Cup a record sixteen times, winning five, and has silver and bronze medals from the Olympics of 1992 and 1996.

Monica Seles

Monica Seles was born in December 1973, in Novi Sad, Yugoslavia. She moved to the USA at just thirteen years of age and by 1991, at seventeen, he became World No. 1, taking over from Steffi Graf. She stayed there until she was stabbed in the shoulder by a fan of Steffi's in a German tournament and was missing from the game for over two years.

Monica Seles won nine Grand Slam titles in an interrupted career that lasted until 2008. Her first was the French at the age of sixteen, and over the period of January 1991 to February

1993, she won thirty-three of the thirty-four tournaments she entered including six Grand Slams. Her career singles' total was 53.

On her return she won the Australian in 1996 but was never quite the same again. Injured in 2003, she stopped playing, although she didn't officially announce her retirement until 2008.

Jennifer Capriati

Jennifer Capriati was even younger than Tracy Austin, just thirteen when she played in a professional tournament in 1990 and actually won in Puerto Rico that same year. Her career was blighted by personal problems, and she took a break before returning to the game in 1996.

She was born in 1976 in New York and three years later was holding a tennis racquet. The family moved to Florida, partly to allow Jennifer to play year-round tennis and be coached by Chris Evert's father. By ten, she was the best player in Lauderhill, woman or man.

At thirteen, she reached the semi-finals of the Virginia Slims, losing to Gabriela Sabatini. She repeated semi-final appearances in Wimbledon and the US in 1991 before defeating Steffi Graf to take Olympic Gold in 1992.

Drink and drugs were her temporary downfall, but she returned to tennis in 1996, still only twenty but with little of her previous spark. Suddenly, in 2001 in Australia, she beat Lindsay Davenport, then Martina Hingis to win a Grand Slam and followed that by winning the French. When she retained her Australian Title, she was World No. 1. That was the highlight and shoulder injuries meant she retired in 2004.

She won fourteen professional tournaments throughout her career.

Martina Hingis

Martina Hingis was born in Slovakia in 1980 but raised in Switzerland. She started to play tennis at a very young age and actually won a Grand Slam doubles title at Wimbledon at only fifteen in 1996, a year after turning professional and the Australian singles in 1997. She went on to win Wimbledon and the US later in the year. She became World No. 1, the youngest in history. She won Australia in the following two years as well as taking each of the Grand Slam doubles at least once.

She initially retired in 2003 because of injury, returned and won the Australian mixed in 2006, but retired again in 2007 after announcing she was under investigation for cocaine use.

While she has not returned to singles, she began to play doubles again in 2013 with some success. She was a losing finalist at the US in the doubles in 2013 before setting up a partnership with Leander Paes that proved extremely fruitful. Together, they won the mixed double Grand Slam, winning the 4th at Roland Garros in 2016. Hingis may have subsequently retired but then she has done that before.

Lindsay Davenport

Davenport was born in 1977 and turned professional at sixteen. She was tall, 1.89m., and powerful with a game well suited to both grass and hard courts and her 50 professional victories is testimony to that. She took gold at the Atlanta Games in 1996 and followed that up with three Grand Slam Championships, the US Open in 1998, Wimbledon in 1999, and the Australian Open in 2000.

She also won doubles at Wimbledon, the US Open and the French. Although she did not officially retire, she announced her pregnancy in 2006, so no one expected her return.

Venus Williams

Venus Williams was born in California in 1980 and learnt her tennis on public courts in Los Angeles. She was already serving a 100 mph by the time she was ten years old, so not surprisingly she had real prospects when she turned professional at just fourteen, having effectively beaten all the junior opposition in the USA.

She still plays on the WTA Tour, and who is to say she won't add to her 46 singles titles. She has a gold medal for Olympic singles in 2000 and three for doubles, as well as seven Grand Slam singles, five being at Wimbledon, and a thirteen doubles with her sister, Serena whom she has faced in eighteen Grand Slam finals.

In 1997, she reached the US Open final, losing to Martina Hingis but in 2000, she won, having already taken the first of her five Wimbledon Titles. Her contract with Reebok signed after that was worth $40m. She retained her titles in 2001.

At the 2000 Olympic Games in Sydney, Australia, Williams captured the gold medal in the singles competition, and then took a second one with Serena in the doubles event. The sisters have credited the other with pushing them in tennis, both as teammates and as competitors. Together, the pair have won thirteen Grand Slam doubles titles and have squared off more than twenty times, including the finals of eight Grand Slam tournaments.

After three doubles golds, the Williams sisters lost in the first round in 2016.

Serena Williams

Serena was born in Saginaw, Michigan, in 1981, and together with older sister, Venus, have arguably changed the game of women's tennis to power and personality. Her first Grand Slam was the US Open in 1999 when she beat Venus, and after returning recently from the birth of her first child, who is to say she will not add to her current total of twenty-three which took her past Steffi Graf's record of twenty-two in the Open Era.

She won the French, Wimbledon, and US Opens in 2002, before winning the 2003 Australian so that she held all four Grand Slams at the same time, though not in the same year. She had a period of injury and slump, partly through lack of motivation, but came back strongly to win three Grand Slams fairly quickly, 2008 US, 2009 Australia, and Wimbledon, then added two more in 2010. She has continued to gather titles in her 30s, and the world awaits what she will do back on the circuit. Grand Slams may be a little early for her in 2018 but who knows?

One of the major differences between Serena and the rest is the prize money Serena has been able to earn during her career. The estimate is $84m, as much as $50m more than any other woman tennis player. Add her endorsements, and it really shows that tennis is now seriously big business. Remember that £25 gift voucher that Billie Jean King won?

Incidentally, she and Venus have six doubles Titles at Wimbledon.

Justine Henin

Justine Henin was born in 1982 in Liège, Belgium, and certainly had a difficult route to the top of tennis including the death of her mother making her, at twelve, the one who had to look after three younger siblings at times and her father's opposition to her relationship with a butcher's son, Pierre Yves, whom she married four years later in 2001. By that time, she had had a very successful junior career and was starting to make an impact amongst the seniors.

She had eight wins in 2003, including the French Open and the US Open, and won the Australian in 2004.

She had a keen rivalry with fellow Belgian Kim Clijsters, with the better of the exchanges over the short time the two played. Her career ended when she announced her retirement, citing wanting to do other things with her life, when she was twenty-five in 2007. She won seven of the seventeen Grand Slam events that she entered while at the peak of her career, had 45 titles and the 2004 Olympic gold. She briefly returned in 2010, but injury soon afterwards led to her permanent retirement

Kim Clijsters

Clijsters was born in Limburg, Belgium, in 1983, the daughter of an international soccer player and national gymnastic champion. She was national junior champion at eleven and decided to concentrate on tennis.

Her professional debut was in 1999, and she won the Masters in 2002. With nine singles wins in 2003, she became World No. 1 (she also won seven doubles). Her first Grand Slam was the US Open in 2005, but she retired to become a wife and mother in 2007. However, in 2009, she returned and won three more Grand Slam singles, the US Open that year when she was unseeded, and she retained the title in 2010. She also regained the No. 1 ranking in 2011 when winning the Australian. Injury caused her withdrawal from Wimbledon and the US, so she retired from competition in 2012 though still played some exhibitions.

Maria Sharapova

Born in Nyagan, Siberia, Russia in 1987, Sharapova was intent on a tennis career at an early age, and as a result went to the USA and the Nick Bollettieri Tennis Academy when she was just nine years old. She turned professional at age fourteen and became the first Russian to win Wimbledon in 2004. It was to take her until 2012 before she won the last of the Grand Slams, the French, and she won that again in 2014.

She became World No. 1 early in 2005, having won the end of season WTA Championship. She won the US Open in 2006, but injuries hampered her progress, though she won the Australian in 2008 before missing some time after shoulder surgery. She won silver in the 2012 Olympics.

She was suspended for two years by the ITF following use of a banned substance, and she has now resumed her career after the term was reduced to fifteen months. However, the highest paid female athlete in 2015 (estimated $29.7m) was no longer a sponsors' dream.

There is a certain level of disquiet about Maria's return so soon. In mitigation, the "drug" she was using had been legal for many years until fairly recently, so who knows the real story because she has been taking it for a decade it seems.

FACTS & FIGURES

1. Conchita Martinez was a clay court specialist and won the Italian Open four times in a row between 1993 and 1996 but could never go on to win the French a few weeks later. She did however win the Wimbledon singles in 1994.

2. Argentina's Gabriela Sabatini reached the French final at fifteen in 1985 and had twenty-seven career singles titles but only one Grand Slam, US in 1990.

3. Anna Kournikova was the first of several Russians to emerge since Olga Morozova in the 70s. She never won a singles Grand Slam, however, despite reaching the Wimbledon semi-final at the first attempt in 1997.

4. The Tour Championships show consistency over a whole season. In 2005, three of the Grand Slam winners, missed the season ending event. The Williams sisters did not get enough points, and Justine Henin- Hardenne, the French Champion, was ill.

5. 1986 does not show on the Australian Championship Trophy because there was no event, as it changed its calendar date to December from January in 1977 and switched back in 1987 when it was played twice.

6. Nine players were ranked No. 1 between the first system in 1973 and the turn of the century. The most weeks in that

spot was Steffi Graf with 378, the least Jennifer Capriati with 3.

7. Althea Gibson was the first Afro-American to win a Grand Slam when she won the French in 1956.

8. There were eight first time winners on the WTA in 2004 with Jelena Jankovic, winner in Budapest, perhaps the best known.

9. Kim Clijsters was the first No. 1 that did not win a Grand Slam during the previous season, 2003.

10. Anastasia Myskina was the first Russian to win a Grand Slam, French 2004.

11. She beat Venus Williams in the quarter finals to end Venus' nineteen match winning run.

12. One title that eluded Martina Navratilova was an Olympic Gold Medal. It was reintroduced in 1988 with the winners in the next four Games when Navratilova may still have had a chance, Steffi Graf, Jennifer Capriati, Lindsay Davenport and Venus Williams.

13. Elena Dementieva reached the 2000 final, a real surprise, and returned in 2008 to win Gold.

14. The first time two defending champions lost in the first round the following year was in 2005; Anastasia Myskina at Paris and Svetlana Kuznetsova in the US.

15. Chris Evert and Martina Navratilova played four French finals, 1975, then three years in a row, 1984-6. Evert won three, only losing in 1985.

16. Kim Clijsters was the lowest ranked player to win an event in WTA Tour history when she won the Sony Ericcson ranked 133 just after returning to the WTA Tour.

17. Monica Seles missed twenty-seven months of tennis after being stabbed in the shoulder at an event. She won the Canadian Open on her return and reached the US final two weeks later.

18. Justin Henin was World No. 1 when she suddenly retired in 2008.

19. Evonne Goolagong's first single title was a Grand Slam, the French in 1971. So was her last, Wimbledon 1980.

20. In January 2011, the top ten players came from ten different countries: Caroline Wozniacki (Denmark), Kim Clijsters (Belgium), Vera Zvonareva (Russia), Francesca Schiavone (Italy), Sam Stosur (Australia), Venus Williams (USA), Li Na (China), Jelena Jankovic (Serbia), Victoria Azarenka (Belarus), Agnieszka Radwanska (Poland).

TRIVIA QUESTIONS

1. Justine Henin retired at the top. How old was she?

   A. 24
   B. 25
   C. 26
   D. 27
   E. 28

2. Who held the record of Grand Slams in the Open Era before Serena Williams reached 23?

   A. Steffi Graf
   B. Martina Navratilova
   C. Venus Williams
   D. Chris Evert
   E. Martina Hingis

3. Where was Martina Hingis born?

   A. Switzerland
   B. Yugoslavia
   C. Czech Republic
   D. Slovenia
   E. Slovakia

4. Who was the youngest player to play in a WTA event?

   A. Tracy Austin
   B. Martina Hingis
   C. Maria Sharapova
   D. Jennifer Capriati
   E. Chris Evert

5. How many Wimbledon singles titles has Martina Navratilova got?

   A. 7
   B. 8
   C. 9
   D. 10
   E. 11

Answer

1. B
2. A
3. E
4. D
5. C

CHAPTER 6
DOUBLES SPECIALISTS

In recent years, the major male tennis players have not played doubles tennis in Grand Slams. It may be a product of "best of five" singles matches, although that was also the case in the middle of the last century when many of the men played.

In some ways, the result has been that doubles has been seen as a specialist event, though the success of the Williams' sisters is obviously an exception. It is worth mentioning some of the established pairs who have had considerable success together. Other than the Williams sisters and the Bryan twins, many of the good doubles players have had more than one partner; Roy Emerson is a prime example of that.

The chapter tends to concentrate more on recent decades when the fields have been larger, but there is some consideration given to a couple of outstanding pairings from well over half a century ago.

Louise Brough Clapp and Margaret Osborne duPont

Brough and duPont won twenty Grand Slam doubles, including twelve at the US Nationals, nine of which were consecutive between 1942 and 1950. They were great friends but also fierce rivals for the singles titles as well. In addition to those twelve US wins, they won five times and Wimbledon and three times in the French. Brough played the ad side, Brough the deuce side.

The Australian title is missing from the CV; they never played there with duPont's husband's health meaning that she never went down to Australia. Brough, however, did win in Australia on her only visit, in the singles, and then with Doris Hart in the doubles.

Seven of their twelve US titles were in straight sets with the closest match being their 5 − 7, 6 − 3, 7 − 5 win against Channing Todd and Doris Hart in 1947.

Brough had eight mixed titles as well, four at Wimbledon, and four the US, but her style wasn't suited to the slow courts of France, so she was unable to capture that singles championship. Margaret duPont did win the French, as well as eight mixed in the US and one at Wimbledon. She won a 13th US doubles with Sarah Palfrey in 1941 before the great partnership with Brough began.

Frank Sedgman and Ken McGregor

The partnership of Australian Frank Sedgman and Ken McGregor was arguably the most successful on the men's doubles circuit for a short time. They won seven of the eight Grand Slams played in 1951 and 1952, thereby obviously doing the Grand Slam in a single season which they did in 1951. No one has ever matched that since. McGregor was a losing finalist at Wimbledon having won the Australian earlier in the year but won the Wimbledon title the following year as well the doubles.

The other claim to fame that the pair had was the longest set in Wimbledon doubles history. It was in defeat however, in 1950. The second set lasted two and a half hours with the US partnership of Gardnar Mulloy and Tony Trabert winning 8 – 6, 8 – 6, 8 – 10, 10 – 8.

Australia was the dominant force in the Davis Cup, and the Sedgman/McGregor partnership made it difficult to beat.

In 1953, the pair turned professional. McGregor's form was never the same again and found both Pancho Segura and Pancho Gonzales too strong.

McGregor's athleticism meant he was not lying when he said all he wanted to do on the professional circuit was to make enough money to return to Australia to play Australian Rules Football, which is what he did.

Lew Hoad and Ken Rosewall

Hoad and Rosewall were great singles players, rivals, and friends. In their time, it was usual to play doubles and mixed as well as in the singles event. Both did this to great effect as a doubles partnership. They won six Grand Slam doubles titles together; two Australia, two Wimbledon, the French, and the US, all coming in the years between 1953 and 1956, thereby completing the career Grand Slam of the four Events.

Hoad won another doubles at Wimbledon in 1955 and the Australian in 1957, with Rex Hartwig and Neale Fraser, respectively. After then winning the Wimbledon singles, Hoad signed a professional contract. Incidentally, he took the mixed at Roland Garros with Mo Connolly in 1954.

Rosewall's singles career was even better; he won three doubles and a mixed as well as those six successes with Hoad. His mixed was the US with Margaret Osborne duPont in 1956, and the two of the three doubles were in the Open Era, the 1968 French and the 1972 Australian. In the decade before the Open Era, Rosewall had also played in the professional ranks.

Margaret Court and Ken Fletcher

It is difficult to find a mixed pairing that played regularly together, especially in the Grand Slam events. There is at least one exception, and that is Margaret Court and Ken Fletcher. They achieved the mixed doubles Grand Slam in 1963, four of eight titles the pair won together; they won Wimbledon three more times and the Australian once.

Fletcher was another of the great Australian men that the country produced through this era, and he had men's titles with Roy Emerson at Roland Garros in 1964 and John Newcombe at Wimbledon in 1966 to add to his CV. He was a very good singles player as well, but the competition in his era was truly fierce. He did win thirty-seven singles titles and reached one Grand Slam final, the Australian in 1963, and lost, you've guessed it, to Roy Emerson.

Court of course, was the top women's player at the time, and her career is summarised in Chapter 4.

Roy Emerson and Fred Stolle

Fred Stolle was actually to make a name for himself in doubles before he teamed up with Roy Emerson. He played with fellow Australian, Bob Hewitt, and won four Grand Slam doubles between 1962 and 1964, two at the Australian and two at Wimbledon. In 1965, he began a partnership with the No. 1 singles player at the time, Roy Emerson, another Australian and they went on to win more doubles Titles. In the first year, they won the French and US, the only two missing from Stolle's CV, then in 1966, the Australian.

While Stolle reached three Wimbledon finals and two Australian, he often found Emerson in the way. He did however win two singles Grand Slams, 1965 at Roland Garros against Tony Roche, and the 1966 US, having beaten Emerson in the semis against Roche's regular doubles partner, John Newcombe. Stolle also took seven mixed Grand Slam titles.

Perhaps doubles was less important to Roy Emerson who took twelve Grand Slam singles titles, but he was a formidable partner for anyone. Or was it less important? He won sixteen Grand Slam doubles to add to those singles titles between 1959 and 1971, including all four of the "majors." He won the French six years in a row, 1960 to 1965, four US, the first in 1959, three Australian and three Wimbledon. Seven of those wins were with Neale Fraser.

John Newcombe and Tony Roche

Tony Roche's game was made for grass, but ironically, his only Grand Slam title was one the slowest surface of all, the clay of Roland Garros where he won in 1966. He was an outstanding doubles player and won fifteen Grand Slams, thirteen of them doubles, five each at the Australian and Wimbledon, two in France, and a single one at the US, all coming between 1965 and 1977. The 1977 win was the Australian when he won with Arthur Ashe, but the other twelve were all partnered by John Newcombe whose impressive singles career is summarized in an earlier chapter.

It was not just in the Grand Slams that the two did so well; their pairing in the Davis Cup was extremely important to Australia, especially in Australian wins in 1965 and 1967. Their best year was 1967 when they won three of the four Grand Slams, missing out at Wimbledon where they went on to win in the next three years, having won it for the first time in 1965.

Roche had two mixed titles, Australian 1966, and Wimbledon 1976, as did Newcombe, the US in 1964 and in 1965, the trophy was shared.

In addition to all his titles with Tony Roche, John Newcombe won Wimbledon in 1966 with Ken Fletcher and four other Grand Slam titles with different partners.

Billie Jean King and Rosie Casals

Billie Jean had a remarkable record across all three games (more on that has been summarised earlier) while although Rosie Casals made two Grand Slam singles finals, she was primarily known for her doubles play and took nine doubles titles and three mixed titles during her career in the Grand Slam events. She reached finals at Australia and France in the doubles, and semis in the mixed at those same venues, but it was at Wimbledon and the US that she excelled.

She won the Wimbledon title five times between 1967 and 1973 and four US, three between 1967 and 1974, and then a final one in 1982. All but the 1982 win were in partnership with Billie Jean King and during that time, they were losing finalists seven times as well. She and King won 56 titles in all, while Casals personal record was 112. They were the only doubles pairing to win on all three surfaces at the US. Wendy Turnbull partnered Casals to the 1982 win.

She won two mixed titles with Ille Nastase at Wimbledon and the US three years later playing with Dick Stockton against King and Fred Stolle.

Ille Nastase and Jimmy Connors

It was not so much the number of titles that this pair won, just two Grand Slams, as the excitement and controversy that they generated on court that warrants their inclusion. Each player individually and as a pair were talking points in the 70s and for long afterwards.

There two wins were at Wimbledon in 1973, the year Nastase had won the French singles and in 1975 at the US. Connors generally concentrated on singles and won eight titles, but even he could not resist the temptation of playing with the exciting Rumanian, and the result was that he had two more Grand Slams to add to his CV.

John McEnroe and Peter Fleming

McEnroe and Fleming won 61 doubles titles of which seven were Grand Slams, four at Wimbledon where McEnroe's deft touch was in its element, and three at the US Open. Fleming did win three singles titles and reached a peak of No. 8 in the World, but it is his partnership with McEnroe for which he is best remembered.

At 6 feet 5 inches, Fleming had plenty of power, and when the two joined together, the effect was devastating. They won seven straight Masters titles between 1978 and 1984 and were never beaten at Madison Square Garden. Their Davis Cup record was 14 – 1, and they played in three Cup winning sides, though their defeat was against Sweden in the final in 1984 which the Swedes went on to win.

Their successes in the Grand Slams were at Wimbledon, 1979, 1981, 1983, and 1984 and at Forest Hills in the US, 1979, 1981, and 1983.

Martina Navratilova and Pam Shriver

Martina Navratilova's career has already been mentioned concentrating on her singles successes, but her partnership with Pam Shriver deserves special mention. A jury would likely pick this pairing as the best women's doubles pairing ever.

Navratilova is the only tennis player, male or female, to have been ranked No. 1 in both the singles and doubles for more than 200 weeks; 332 in singles, 237 in doubles. She has thirty-one Grand Slam doubles titles, five before the Open Era, and twenty-six after it began. Initially, she played with Chris Evert and then Billie Jean King, winning regularly but then she teamed up with Pam Shriver in 1981. They won twenty Grand Slams together, including one in the calendar year, 1984.

They were four wins at the Australian and the French, five at Wimbledon and seven down in Australia. At one point they won 109 matches in a row and have ten WTA World doubles, won in eleven years between 1981 and 1992.

They actually lost their first final, the Australian in 1981 against Kathy Jordan and Anne Smith, but were only to lose twice against in finals, the 1985 Wimbledon and US Opens.

Todd Woodbridge and Mark Woodforde

The Australian duo of Todd Woodbridge and Mark Woodforde won eleven Grand Slams, as well as the gold medal at the Atlanta Olympics in 1996, taking silver four years later in Sydney. They had formed a partnership in 1991 and played together for the rest of the decade before Woodforde retired. Todd Woodbridge continued to play and had further success playing with Jonas Bjorkman, winning five more titles before Woodbridge retired as well in 2005.

Woodbridge had been a Top 20 singles player before partnering up with Mark Woodforde; the partnership won 61 ATP World Tour titles in its years. In addition, they were a formidable pairing in the Australian Davis Cup side. They won Wimbledon five years in a row between 1993 and 1997. He once reached the Wimbledon singles semi-finals, losing to Pete Sampras, but did win two ATP Singles titles.

They still play the occasion exhibition while Woodbridge played in the mixed with Kim Clijsters in the Australian Open; he won each of the mixed Grand Slams in his career, the US three times.

The Bryan Brothers

American twins Bob and Mike Bryan held the top doubles ranking for 483 weeks. They have won more Grand Slams and other majors and tournaments than any other pair. If you add the Olympic gold at London in 2012, there is nothing missing from their CVs. In addition, Bob has won seven mixed and Mike four.

When they won at Wimbledon in 2013, they held every Grand Slam and the Olympic Gold at one time.

Their 112 titles from a total of 167 finals is an impressive statistic, and even at 39 years old, they hold the World No. 2 ranking, twenty-two years after first turning professional and fifteen years after their success really began. They finished as runners-up at the Australian in 2018 as they approach 40.

They finally retired from Davis Cup tennis last year after competing for fourteen years. With such a strong doubles pairing, any tie with involves reverse singles and is the first country to three to win, is bound to be strong if the doubles pairing is difficult to beat. US Singles tennis has not been that strong, but USA won the Cup beating Russia in the final with the Bryan brothers winning. Their overall Cup record is 24 – 5.

Leander Paes and Mahesh Bhupathi

The outstanding India pair of Leander Paes and Mahesh Bhupathi have been great performers in doubles, both as a pair and in mixed competition as well. Few tennis players from India have reached the top, though the Amritraj Brothers, Vijay and Anand, played on the circuit in the 1970s.

These days, there are official rankings, and Paes and Bhupathi reached the No 1. ranking, despite not winning as many titles as many of the "old greats." Their best spell was between 1997 and 2002, and they had a brief reunion in 2011, but their relationship has never been a smooth one.

Paes is still playing in his mid-40s, and his doubles and mixed Grand Slam records are impressive. Paes won in Australia with Wayne Arthurs as a scratch pair due to injuries. As a pair, Paes and Bhupathi won Wimbledon and Roland Garros in 1999 and Roland Garros again in 2002. Paes himself has gone on to win the US in 2006 with Martin Damm, the 2009 with Lucas Dlohy, followed by wins with Radek Stepanek in Australia in 2012, and the 2013 US to make eight Grand Slams in all in men's doubles. He turned his attention to the mixed, where partnered at times by another veteran, Martina Hingis, he was won ten titles including a Grand Slam in all four events when they won in Paris in 2016.

Natasha Zvereva and Gigi Fernandez

Zvereva and Fernandez have only the pairing of Martina Navratilova and Pam Shriver in front of them in terms of titles. Natasha Zvereva from Belarus was a successful youngster winning Wimbledon Girls' singles 1986 and the US Open Girls' in 1987. The following year, she was a losing finalist in the French Open and actually beat both Steffi Graf and Monica Seles in the same event, Wimbledon 1998.

It was in doubles though that she made her name. She had already won three tour titles when she teamed up with Puerto Rican-American Gigi Fernandez and went on a nine-title winning streak; at Wimbledon 1993, they held the four Grand Slam Championships. In total they won fourteen of their seventeen Slam finals.

They began in France in 1992, when Zvereva had already won titles and went on to win the next four titles as well, but defeat at the US meant they did not complete the calendar Grand Slam. However, they won three again the following year, failing again in the US. In 1995, they won the US for the first time, retaining it the next year, and eventually made it six from seven in France. Zvereva won once more after the partnership finished; with Martina Hingis in the 1997 in the Australia. She won two mixed as well, the Australian in 1990 and 1995.

For her part, Gigi had won the US with Robin White and the French with Jana Novotna before they teamed up and controversially decided to represent the USA in Olympics, winning gold in 1992 and 1996 with Mary Jo Fernandez. She explained she did so because Puerto Rico did not have another female player of any quality.

The Williams Sisters

There are several remarkable things about the Williams sisters, not least the number of singles titles they have accumulated while also being the dominant force in Grand Slam doubles.

Venus' singles success, including five Wimbledons and Olympic singles gold in 2000, was fairly early in her career while Serena's Grand Slam singles titles are rising all the time. Their careers are summarised elsewhere, but it is worth highlighting their doubles success together.

They won golds for the doubles in Sydney, Beijing, and London. Add to that the thirteen Grand Slam doubles:

Australia in 2001, 2003, 2009, and 2010
French in 1999 and 2010
Wimbledon in 2000, 2002, 2008, 2009, 2012, and 2016.
US in 2009.

There is a chance they made add to that figure, though if Serena misses most of the 2018 season, that becomes less likely.

FACTS & FIGURES

1. Manuel Santana was the first Spaniard to win a Grand Slam singles when he won the French in 1961. He went on to win it again in 1964, the US in 1965, and Wimbledon in 1966. He was the only non-Australian to be part of Roy Emerson's remarkable sixteen doubles titles, partnering him to the French at Roland Garros in 1963.

2. Nicola Pietrangeli is considered the best male tennis player Italy has produced, although he was born in Tunisia. He won two French titles as well as the doubles in 1959 with Orlando Sirola beating Emerson and Fraser, having won the mixed the season before with Australian Shirley Bloomer.

3. Ion Tiriac was born in Transylvania, Rumania, in 1939 and played ice hockey as well as tennis. He won twenty-three titles in the Open Era, twenty-two being doubles, but his only Grand Slam was the French in 1970 when he and Ille Nastase beat Arthur Ashe and Charlie Pasarell in straight sets.

4. Mats Wilander had a fine Grand Slam singles record with seven titles between 1983 and 1988, though he never went past the quarter finals at Wimbledon, except in the doubles where he and fellow Swede, Joakim Nystrom, took the Championship in 1986

5. Dutchman Tom Okker won thirty-one singles titles and spent seven consecutive years in the Top 10 rankings, but it is for his doubles' successes, 78 Titles, that he is best remembered. Included in those is the French with John Newcombe in 1973, the US with Marty Reissen in 1976, and the WCT World doubles in 1978 with Wojtek Fibak.

6. Martina Hingis and Anna Kournikova won sixteen WTA titles in their short time together, including two Australian Opens in 1999 and 2002.

7. Hana Mandlikova won the first of her four Grand Slam singles titles at seventeen, the 1980 Australian. She had to wait until the end of the decade to get her name on a doubles trophy, the 1989 US, playing with Martina Navratilova. She retired the following year and began coaching Jana Novotna, a future Wimbledon Champion in the making who sadly died in 2017 at the age of 49.

8. In the days of big hitters, Italian Sara Errani has proved you can still succeed. She has five Grand Slam doubles titles, amongst her twenty-five titles in all. She and Roberta Vinci, who also has twenty-three doubles titles, have been a great partnership. The two won the French, US, two Australian, and Wimbledon between 2012 and 2014.

9. Martina Hingis has had an interrupted career. Her singles exploits are mentioned in Chapter 5, but her doubles record is truly remarkable. She is the current holder of the

US mixed with Jamie Murray, and since her return to the circuit in 2013, purely to play doubles, she has just retired with twenty Grand Slam titles, ten since 2013.

10. Andy Murray has reached World No. 1 and won three Grand Slam singles titles. Older brother Jamie has five spread across men's doubles and mixed. It is only in the Davis Cup that the two have played together.

11. Stan Smith helped the USA to seven Davis Cup wins as well as reaching thirteen Grand Slam doubles finals, winning on five occasions, each of those wins with Bob Lutz although he played with others in some of those final appearances. The wins were four at the US where he also won the singles in 1971, and one at the Australian in 1970, the year before he won the Wimbledon singles title.

12. Helena Sukova was ranked the best female doubles player in 1990. Her record justifies that; nine Doubles including all the Grand Slams, and five mixed with the Australian, the only one missing from the CV.

13. Michael Stich beat his compatriot Boris Becker to win at Wimbledon in 1991 but then combined with him to won Olympic Gold in 1992, having also won the Wimbledon doubles with John McEnroe that year in a five-hour marathon.

14. South African Cliff Drysdale was one of the driving forces

behind the Open Era and was the first president of the ATP. His sole Grand Slam title was the men's doubles in the 1972 US, partnered by Brit Roger Taylor, defeating John Newcombe and Owen Davidson.

15. Rafael Osuna has been described as the "Best Player You Never Knew." He is undoubtedly the best player to come out of Mexico and won the US in 1963 and three doubles, the first with American Dennis Ralston, and the other two with fellow countryman Antonio Palafox, Wimbledon in 1960 and 1963, and the US in 1962. He was sadly killed in a plane crash in 1969 when still only 30.

16. After partnering Osuna in 1960, Ralston had four more doubles wins, three at the US and the final one in 1966 in the French, the American titles with Chuck McKinley, and the French with Clark Graebner.

17. Francoise Durr was known more for her doubles than singles but did capture one singles title, the French in 1967. In doubles, she won the French five times and the US twice, as well as being runner-up at Wimbledon six times. Gail Chanfreau was her partner for the first three French titles and Ann Hayden Jones for the other two. She won the US with Darlene Hard and then Betty Stove. Jean-Claude Barclay was her partner for three French mixed and Tony Roche for her 1976 Wimbledon success.

18. Ann Hayden Jones had her only Wimbledon singles success

in 1969, but she won Grand Slam titles in the women's doubles, the French three times where she had also taken the singles twice, the mixed in Australia (1969), which was shared because of bad weather, and Wimbledon the same year with Fred Stolle.

19. Angela Mortimer Barrett won three Grand Slam titles (the US eluded her) but also won the Wimbledon doubles early in her career, 1955, with Jacqueline Shilcock in an all-British final.

20. Angela and her husband John are just one of two married couples in the Hall of Fame; Steffi Graf and Andre Agassi are the other.

TRIVIA QUESTIONS

1. Who did a Grand Slam of the four men's doubles events between 1953 and 1956?

   A. Lew Hoad and Ken Rosewall

   B. Roy Emerson and Neal Fraser

   C. Roy Emerson and Fred Stolle

   D. John Newcombe and Tony Roche

   E. John McEnroe and Peter Fleming

2. Leander Paes did a mixed Grand Slam with which woman?

   A. Martina Navratilova

   B. Rosie Casals

   C. Martina Hingis

   D. Pam Shriver

   E. Gigi Fernandez

3. Who did Tony Roche win his only mixed title with?

   A. Margaret Court

   B. Billie Jean King

   C. Rosie Casals

   D. Anne Smith

   E. Francoise Durr

4. How many men's doubles titles did Roy Emerson win?

   A. 15

   B. 16

   C. 17

   D. 18

   E. 19

5. Who can probably claim to be the best women's doubles pairing ever?

   A. Billie Jean King & Rosie Casals

   B. Natasha Zvereva & Gigi Fernandez

   C. The Williams Sisters

   D. Martina Navratilova & Pam Shriver

   E. Louise Brough Clapp & Margaret Osborne duPont

Answers

1. A
2. C
3. E
4. B
5. D

CHAPTER 7

AROUND THE WORLD OF TENNIS

Tennis is far more than the top professionals playing in Grand Slams. Over the years, top players have competed in events such as the Davis Cup and the Fed Cup wherever they can fit it into their schedule. Certainly, years ago, the top men played in doubles and mixed on a regular basis, but that is less the case today.

Tennis involves more than just the players. The Hall of Fame holds most of the players who have retired and are mentioned in this book, but there are other notables that have received that honour. Coaches have developed young talent, and their contribution is recognised. There have been junior championships for years, but all four Grand Slams now embrace them, usually during the second week when the singles events have just sixteen players remaining from the 128 first round entrants so courts are more readily available.

Wheelchair tennis has been a great innovation, and its story is told here.

Davis Cup

On February 9, 1900, Dwight Filley Davis challenged British tennis players to come to the USA to play against his Harvard team, and he produced a solid silver trophy for the winners. The US National Lawn Tennis Association approved his idea, and he spent $750 on getting the trophy produced. Great Britain was regarded as the world's top tennis nation at that time and sent a three-man team over to play over three days in a format retained to this day; four singles and one doubles in the middle. Rain ruined one of the days, but Harvard, representing the USA, had already won 3 − 0. This match began a history that has continued to this day.

By 1904, it was a Cup which other countries sought so the competition expanded with initially Belgium and France, followed by Australia and New Zealand entered.

Once it was expanded, there was no looking back other than the War year. Initially, France, Austria, Belgium, and Australasia, a combined Australia/New Zealand team, took part and by the 1920s, there were twenty countries involved. The USA, GB, and Australasia were the dominant forces until the late 1920s when France produced some fine players to win the Cup six times; Jean Borotra, Jacques Brugnon, Henri Cochet and Rene Lacoste. Normal service was then resumed with Australia especially strong through the 60s.

By the time the Open Era arrived, there were fifty nations

playing in the Cup, and in 1972, the idea of the challenge round was scrapped; the holders had had a bye to the final, playing whomever emerged from the knockout competition. Every country was then to play every round from the start. Another milestone that year was the Italian Nicola Pietrangeli playing for Italy for the last time; 164 games and 120 wins.

There was a new name on the Cup in 1974, South Africa with Sweden, Italy, and Czechoslovakia winning in the next years.

The World Group of sixteen was introduced in 1981 with zone groups below and promotion and relegation. NEC Sponsorship meant prize money was introduced as well.

Sweden and Germany both had three wins in the 80s and in 1993, the Cup had 100 countries competing.

It has been difficult for all the top players to commit to playing in the Davis Cup each year, so busy is the ATP calendar, but all the 21st Century greats have appeared for their countries and won— Roger Federer, Rafael Nadal, Novak Djokovic, and Andy Murray.

The first round losers in the world group stage have to play-off to retain their places in the Group for the following year against the winners in the zone group below. The champions are the team that win the knockout competition itself.

Federation Cup

The original idea of a team competition dates back to 1919, the idea of Hazel Hotchkiss Wightman, but it was rejected. As a result, she gave a trophy to be played for between the USA and Great Britain.

The Wightman Cup began in 1923 at a time when the USA and Great Brain were the two strongest women's tennis nations. It ran until 1989, and effectively lost any appeal because Great Britain could no longer compete with the strength of the USA. It had been played alternately in the two countries every year, except the War years but in that time, Britain had only won ten times in 61 matches. The last Cup, in Williamsburg Virginia, was the 11th in a row when the USA had won and six of those had been 7 – 0, the format being five singles and two doubles.

Its passing was sad for those keen on history but it no longer seemed to have any validity.

It was many years after it was first proposed when Nell Hopman took up the idea of an Internations Cup. The competition was born in 1963, the 50th anniversary of the ITF (originally ILTF) to be played each year over a week, in a different venue each year.

The first Cup had sixteen entrants with all the top players in the world taking part. USA defeated Australia at Queen's Club, London, and subsequently they have won the Cup eighteen times in all with the Czech Republic (five as Czechoslovakia) second with ten and Australia third on seven.

There was no appearance money paid, but significant sponsorship helped the Cup expand. By the mid-1990s, 73 countries competed with regional qualifying competitions introduced. The name was shortened to the Fed Cup and in 1995 became a mixed competition.

The current format is a world group of eight, a second tier of eight and three regional groups with promotion and relegation. Each tie is home and away over three weekends.

World Team Tennis

World Team Tennis (WTT) began in 1974, mixed teams representing USA cities or States.

Back then, Billie Jean King had taken a stand against different prize money in Grand Slam events, and she won. This new concept was to confirm tennis as a two-sex sport. The Denver Racquets beat the Philadelphia Freedoms to become the first Champions with other teams including the Los Angeles Strings', Pittsburgh Triangles, and in 1975, the Boston Lobsters.

Martina Navratilova celebrated twenty seasons in WTT in 2009; all the "greats" have played in it at one time or another; Andy Roddick as a 17-year-old played for Idaho Sneakers, Steffi Graf in 2005 after retiring from competition years in 1999, Martina Hingis for New York Sportstime also in 2005, Kim Clijsters in 2009 before going on to win the US Open.

Sacramento Capitals had a winning streak between 1997 and 2000, which Washington Kastles, led by Venus Williams, beat with wins from 2011 until 2015.

Subsequently Orange County Aviators and San Diego Breakers have played in the finals, San Diego winning in 2016 and Orange County getting revenge the year after.

World Tennis Challenge

The Australian Open opens the years calendar but not until after the World Tennis Challenge, which is a professional exhibition tennis tournament held over three nights in Adelaide the week before. It began in 2009, the idea of a number of former players including Jim Courier and Mark Woodforde.

Team Australia this year was Mark Philippoussis, Thanasi Kokkinakis, John Peers, Mansour Bahrami, and Henri Kontinen. Sixty players have played in the World Tennis Challenge since it began, and they include eleven former World No. 1s and thirty-five who were once in the top ten. Add to that the quality of the doubles' players, nine No. 1s and quality is guaranteed. Henri Leconte has played seven times with Mansour Bahrami and Mats Wilander on six each.

The total Grand Slam titles among players is currently 69 singles titles, 90 doubles, and 49 mixed.

Nine countries were involved in the latest challenge; Australia, Brazil, Cyprus, Finland, France, GB, Iran, Sweden and the USA.

The Tiers below the Main Tour

The ATP soon had a large membership and its role was clearly to improve the opportunities for all its members. In 1978, the launch of the Challenger Tour for the second tier of professionals did precisely that.

That first season, there were eighteen events, beginning in January in Auckland and then Hobart, resuming in June after the clay court season was over.

Moving to the present day, there are 155 events on the Challenger Tour, in all corners of the world. The prize money ranges from $50,000 to $150,000.

The Champions Tour is for those whose best playing days may be behind them but they do still mean that spectators are able to see their favourites, even if they are a little slower than they were in their prime.

The WTA 125K series started in 2012 for women below the elite level of professionals. It has a current calendar of eleven events, ten of which have a prize fund of £125,000, with the Oracle Challenger providing $150,000.

Championship Finals at the Season End

There are high profile ATP events throughout the year and the titles are highly prized by winners, if not quite as highly as the Grand Slams. They form the basis of the points that players accumulate over the season. Within the season, there are nine Master events that have a higher standing than the other events during the year, other than the Grand Slams.

The ATP World Tour Masters 1000 is the current name for those nine events that the ATP places the most importance upon, after the Grand Slams and the end of season Championships. They earn players more points than the other events so success in these nine certainly help players to qualify for those end of season championships.

Originally, these events were known as the "ATP Championship Series, Single Week" from 1990 until sponsorship resulted in a change of name; the "Mercedes-Benz Super 9". In 2000, there was another change, firstly to the "TennisMasters Series" and then changed to "ATP Masters Series."

Each year, there are four Masters 1000 held in Europe, four in North America, and one in Asia. The world's leading players have usually dominated the top events, and certainly that is the case today. Roger Federer, Rafa Nadal, Novak Djokovic, and Andy Murray have certainly done so.

The so-called "Big 4" won seventeen consecutive events from 2010 until the 2012 Masters and won all in 2013. It has only been injury and absence that has changed that dominance a little. Nadal has obviously been the man to beat on clay; Monte Carlo, Madrid, Rome, and Hamburg. Rome and Monte Carlo are the two that Federer has not won. The North American events are on hard court; Indian Wells, Miami, Canada, Cincinnati, as is the Shanghai event, and in these Federer and Djokovic have done far better than Nadal who has also won seven, the omissions being Miami and Paris.

Ivan Lendl won all nine of these years before they became so prominent and Djokovic is just a USA Event short of matching him.

The top eight at the year-end then play in the ATP World Championships in two leagues of four in a round robin system with the winners of one group playing the runner up in the other and vice versa in semi-finals.

There is a doubles championship run on the same basis.

Since 2009, the championship finals have been held at the O2 Arena in London when Nikolay Davydenko beat Juan Martin del Potro. Roger Federer won in the next two years to reach a record seven titles but has not won since. Novak Djokovic won four in a row from there but was deprived of a fifth by Andy Murray. The current holder is Gregor Dmitrov, who beat Belgian David Goffin in the final.

The WTA runs a similar system with events running throughout the season. Caroline Wozniacki beat Venus Williams to win in 2017, eight years since her last title. Wozniacki incidentally finally won her first Grand Slam a few weeks later, beating Simone Halep of Rumania in the 2018 Australian Open, and in the process became World No. 1 again.

Wheelchair Tennis

The origins of wheelchair tennis followed a meeting between an acrobat skier, Brad Parks, just eighteen at the time, and a wheelchair athlete Jeff Minnenbraker. Parks had become a paraplegic himself after a serious injury, and the two talked about the viability of tennis for those in wheelchairs. That was half a century ago.

They began to promote it on the USA's West Coast, and soon there was a set of rules and a tennis tournament. By 1980, a circuit of ten tournaments was in place across the USA and the first US Open in Irvine which Parks won. By the end of that year, there were 300 players, so it was logical to form a Players Association (WTPA). The US Open in October became the culmination of a season-long circuit, and the first overseas competitor emerged; Frenchman Jean Pierre Limborg. His enthusiasm once he returned to Paris was the catalyst for a club in Paris and another started in Australia.

Top French players helped the process in France; doubles between an able-bodied player partnered by a wheelchair player. The biggest manufacturer of wheelchairs in the world, Everest & Jennings, joined up in 1984, and play began in Japan and the UK. In 1985, there were now forty events and around 1,500 players in the USA.

A World Team Cup followed, and in 1986 the French Open and over in the USA, the first Junior Championship was held in 1986.

The growth had been rapid in just a decade. It was logical that the ITF got involved, and at its 1988 AGM, the rules were formally adopted.

In 1989, the first Australian Open was held and with sponsorship from NEC, prize money, a tour and ranking was possible. In 1992, wheelchair tennis was an event in the Paralympics in Barcelona.

The Brad Parks Award has become an annual trophy in recognition of his contribution to the game. He was the first winner of what was then the IWTF Trophy, later renamed. In 1998, the IWTF became fully integrated into the ITF and is disbanded to be replaced by the International Wheelchair Tennis Association (IWTA).

The Australian Open in 2002 was the first occasion when the wheelchair event ran parallel to the main event and by 2007, all four Grand Slams did the same thing.

To date, each Olympics saw keener competition and greater numbers; London 2012 was the best yet. There were 112 competitors from thirty-one countries, and happily, Rio managed to almost match that in 2016. The future is bright.

Junior Grand Slams

While they don't get the publicity afforded to the main event, each of the Grand Slams also run junior equivalents, generally in the second week of the tournament. That began back in 1977 though national championships had been a feature of tennis for half a century before that. There are five other events for Juniors to play that can earn them ranking points.

A glance at the lists of former winners will show you many of the great names of tennis, men and women. Recent winners come from all parts of the Globe including Taipei, China, Ukraine, Hungary, Australia, North America, and Spain. It shows how effectively the Game of Tennis has been spread right across the world. There are four events each time, singles and doubles, boys and girls, with no plans to introduce a mixed competition at this stage.

The five Grade "A" events for 2018 show how important the organisers feel it is to take tournaments to different parts of the world. They are scheduled for Mexico, Brazil, the USA, Italy, and Japan. Similar to the Main Tours, there is a Masters at the end of each season; they have been run since 2015, and the eight qualifiers are those who have accumulated the most points from the season's competitions.

Hall of Fame

It would be an impossible task to include everyone who has made a contribution to coaching and mentoring in tennis. Today's top professionals have a team of several people looking after their interests, everything from coaching and general health to mentoring and psychology. There are four men who are in the Hall of Fame for their contributions at different times during the history of golf, and each deserves a mention:

- Nick Bollettieri was a high school football quarterback, a paratrooper in the army, and even a law school student for five months at the University of Miami. He played a single year of collegiate tennis at Spring Hill College in Mobile, Alabama. He actually began to teach tennis for $1.50 a half hour at North Miami Tennis Courts to fund his studies. As his reputation grew, so did his price— $6. His first real success was Brian Gottfried, who got to World No. 3 in 1977.

  He co-founded the Port Washington (N.Y.) Tennis Academy, whose pupils included Vitas Gerulaitis and John McEnroe. It was in 1976, when he was already forty-five that he took a teaching job at the Colony Beach and Tennis Resort, Sarasota, Florida. The Nick Bollettieri Tennis Academy began the next year with his students living in his house. He borrowed $1m from a friend in 1980 to build on land used for growing tomatoes in Bradenton.

  He went on to teach an impressive list of players, including many future Grand Slam winners; Andre Agassi, Boris Becker, Jim Courier, Martina Hingis, Jelena Jankovic, Marcelo Rios, Monica Seles, Maria Sharapova, and Serena and Venus Williams. In addition, other players have used his expertise to help develop their games: Jimmy Arias, Carling Bassett, Thomas Enqvist, Brad Gilbert, Brian Gottfried, Anna Kournikova, Mary Pierce, and Mark Phillippousis. There's more but this is enough to illustrate the impact this effectively non-playing tennis man could develop talent.

He sold up to Mark McCormack and IMG in 1987 with the complex of more than 400 acres now working in eight sports.

- Harry Hopman is a legend of Australian tennis, and it is not for the two Grand Slam doubles and four mixed, as well as the mixed in the US that he won in the 1930s. He played in three Davis Cups as well. That would not have got him in the Hall of Fame. Between 1950 and 1967, Australia won the Davis Cup fifteen times, and remember several of its players turned professional after winning Grand Slams so each of them needed replacing. Hopman captained the Davis Cup side for twenty-two years in all.

He was a self-confessed disciplinarian who turned out several extremely intense and disciplined players. He set standards and expected his players to behave to them, down to dress, appearance in general, diet, and curfews. Nor did he tolerate any indiscipline on the tennis court and was happy to fine players who broke any of his "rules."

The names that have a debt of gratitude to Hopman reads like a "Who's Who" of tennis greats: Frank Sedgman, Ken McGregor, Lew Hoad, Ken Rosewall, Rod Laver, Neale Fraser, John Newcombe, Tony Roche, Roy Emerson, Fred Stolle. The list goes on.

His players were fit; they ran five miles each morning before practise began.

In the 1950s, Aussies were successful in twenty-one of the Grand Slam singles events, and there were fourteen finals where both finalists were Hopman's boys. The achievements of those mentioned are summarised elsewhere in this book. Suffice to say, it was an astonishing era.

He went to the USA in 1971 and coached some bright young talent there as well.

- Vic Braden was encouraged to play tennis by an employee of Monroe, Michigan, who caught him stealing tennis balls that flew over the fence. It was the best thing he ever did. He quickly emerged as a talent and won a scholarship to Kalamazoo College.

The legacy that Braden has left tennis is a whole raft of tennis players, casual to champions, as well as a host of people capable of passing on the message as well.

In the 1950s, he was a tennis teacher and basketball coach in Toledo, Ohio. During the winter, he went to Southern California, teaching tennis in Beverly Hills and Palm Springs, including to Hollywood stars Lana Turner and Debbie Reynolds. In 1955, he settled permanently in Southern California, and he was hired as a janitor and sixth grade teacher. During the three years he spent there, Vic Braden earned a Master's in Educational Psychology.

He had met Jack Kramer in 1953, and Kramer realised his abilities at promotion. He had occasionally played tennis, but his skills with the media were far better. He was a good observer, watching the best players and how they played particular shots.

In 1960, he saw some land in a suburb of Los Angeles, and within a year, it was the Jack Kramer Club where Braden quickly made a name for himself as a teacher. They employed a woman called Jeanne Austin who had four children. Very soon, she was pregnant with a fifth, born a girl and called Tracy. Braden taught this young girl from the age of two, and in 1992, she entered the Hall of Fame.

Brady wrestled with the issue of the best way to teach tennis, and in the early 1970s, he devised the concept of a tennis college where every modern technique could be used in coaching. He never lost his interest in breaking new boundaries, and for two decades more, his life was about videos, seminars, books, and research.

- Dr. Robert Walter Johnson went to Lincoln University in Pennsylvania and became coach and mentor to two tennis players who made history, the first African-American Wimbledon Champions, Althea Gibson and Arthur Ashe. Johnson made it his aim to develop African Americans wherever and whenever he could.

He founded the Junior Development Programme for them through the American Tennis Association (ATA).

Johnson entered the Virginia Sports Hall of Fame in 1972, the Mid-Atlantic Tennis Hall of Fame in 1988, and finally the International Tennis Hall of Fame in 2009. Other honours he received were being named the NAACP Life Membership Chairman and receiving the Spiro T. Agnew Honorary Citizenship Award.

His house and tennis court is an historic home located in Lynchburg, Virginia. It was built in 1911 and was put on to the National Register of Historic Places in 2002.

Pro Circuit before the Open Era

There was a small pool of professionals in the years after the second World War who had had successful amateur careers but then decided to turn professional, often out of necessity. The amateur regulations were strict, but it was still the Grand Slams that received the most attention, even if good marketing attracted crowds to games between the top professionals.

What the professional circuit lacked was a dynamic because of the regular clashes between the same players. It is a needless exercise to talk about who were the better players. Rod Laver did the Grand Slam before he turned professional and did it again after the Open Era was announced, so he was certainly someone that would have changed Grand Slam records through the 60s, as would Ken Rosewall and perhaps the older Pancho Gonzales.

Pancho Gonzales

While Richard "Pancho" Gonzales won just two Grand Slam singles and two doubles, his name should always be considered when discussing the best ever male tennis player. Jack Kramer ran a professional circuit, and he joined in 1949 at twenty-one years old after just playing for three years as an amateur. He played on the professional circuit until the Open Era, which he embraced. When he finally retired, he had 100 titles in twenty-five years.

In 1969, his first round match against Charlie Pasarell at Wimbledon lasted 5 hours 12 minutes over two days before the 41-year-old succumbed 22-24, 1-6, 16-14, 6-3, 11-9.

He was born and grew up in Los Angeles and taught himself to play. He won two US National Men's singles championships (1948-49), two US Clay Court singles (1948-49), the US Indoor singles (1949), and the US Indoor mixed doubles in 1949, as well the 1949 Wimbledon and French doubles championships. As a pro, he won fifteen major championships, including eight US Pro Championship to reach World No. 1 ranking which he held from 1952 to 1960.

Pancho Segura

Francisco "Pancho" Segura from Ecuador who joined Jack Kramer's circuit after a brief amateur career and played professionally from 1947 for twenty years. He was born in Guayaquil, one of seven children in a poor family. It was a logical move to take advantage of the talent he had.

He won tournaments throughout Latin America as a teenager, and the US player Gardnar Mulloy, who was coaching the University of Miami tennis team, offered him a scholarship; he won three straight NCAA singles between 1943 and 1945.

He played in Europe and did win the 1944 US Clay Court title and the 1946 Indoor but turned professional the next year for obvious reasons. He became a better player as a pro as he learned the game and won the US Pro three years in a row, 1950 – 52 as well as 3 US doubles. He played his last US Pro in 1962 at forty-one and his last US Open at Forest Hills in 1970 as he approached fifty. Later, he became a teacher of the game with his star pupil being Jimmy Connors.

Jack Kramer

Jack Kramer was world No. 1 in 1946 but never saw amateur tennis as a sustainable lifestyle. He was the driving force behind setting up a professional circuit in 1947, using venues such as Madison Square Garden. Twenty-five years later, he was central to the formation of the Association of Tennis Professionals (ATP).

He grew up in Los Angeles and at fifteen, in 1936, he won the National Boys, followed by the National Junior in 1938. His reward a year later was selection for the US Davis Cup side, playing in the doubles with Joe Hunt. Years later, in 1946 and 1947, he won all his singles as USA beat Australia to take the Cup.

He won ten major titles; three at the US Nationals (1946, 1947), Wimbledon (1947) and doubles titles in the US Nationals (1940, 1941, 1943, 1947) and Wimbledon (1946, 1947) as well as the mixed in the US Nationals (1941).

At the end of 1947, Kramer turned professional with Chicago promoter Jack Harris funding a match between Kramer and Bobby Riggs. He beat Riggs again in the 1948 US Pro 3-6, 6-3, and the 1949 Wembley Pro over Riggs, 2-6, 6-4, 6-3, 6-4. He advanced to the 1950 French Pro final.

His drive lead to innovation throughout his life and many have a debt to him for what was achieved.

Tony Trabert

Tony Trabert was born in Cincinnati, and by the age of eleven was already showing great promise, developing his game on clay courts in the park close to home. He went to Ohio State and won the NCAA in 1951.

He was World No. 1 in 1953 and 1955, winning five Grand Slam singles and five doubles. He won successive French in 1954 and 1955, two US in 1953 and 1955, and Wimbledon in 1955, three in a single year. The closest he got to the Australian was the 1955 semi-finals when he lost to Ken Rosewall. He turned professional at the end of that season. His doubles titles were three French, a single US, and Australian.

He won thirteen US titles in singles and doubles on all four surfaces: grass, indoor, clay court, and hard court, and played Davis Cup between 1951 and 1955, captaining the side from 1976 to 1980, winning twice.

Explaining his decision to turn professional, he said he had a wife and two children. He had received a £10 voucher for winning Wimbledon! He made $125,000 in a 14-month period, playing in 101 matches.

Lew Hoad

Lew Hoad's amateur career lasted for six years, 1951 until 1957, before he turned professional. He reached twenty-three Grand Slam Finals across the three "styles" winning in thirteen; singles wins were 1956 Australia, France, and Wimbledon, but he was beaten at the US by Ken Rosewall whom he had beaten in both the Australian and at Wimbledon.

He won six doubles with his friend and rival, Rosewall, and in all won eight—three Australia, three Wimbledon, and one each at Roland Garros and the US. He won the French mixed with Mo Connolly as well. Beating Ashley Cooper to take his second Wimbledon title in 1957, he was given a $125,000 signing on fee to go professional that year.

He won the Davis Cup in three of the four years he played, 1953 – 56, and finished with a 17 – 4 record. He lived in Spain in retirement but died from leukaemia at only 59.

FACTS & FIGURES

1. Butch Buchholtz, who joined the pro tour in 1961, as Pancho Segura's was coming to the end of his top playing days said of him: "Nobody had a better tennis mind. I have a good understanding of the sport because of Pancho."

2. Billie Jean King called Pancho Segura "The Ph.D. of Tennis."

3. Vic Seixas played in a record twenty-eight US National/Open tournaments, spanning from 1940 to 1969. He won the singles title in 1954.

4. At the 1966 US Nationals, at 43-year-old he was the oldest player in the field, and he beat a 19-year-old Stan Smith, 6-3, 6-4, 2-6, 2-6, 6-4. Smith was later to win the Wimbledon title.

5. Frank Sedgman's 80th birthday celebrations had a surprise guest when Jack Kramer flew over from Los Angeles to join in. Australian Sedgman won seventeen Grand Slam doubles titles but also five singles between 1949 and 1952 before turning professional with Kramer's circuit. He also won each of the mixed Slams with Doris Hart.

6. San Marino's Dominico Vicini has the most Davis Cup appearances; 93. He was 61 wins from 135 games played.

7. In 2015, when GB won the Davis Cup, Andy Murray had an 8 – 0 singles record.

8. Tut Bartzen played for the USA between 1952 and 1961. He won all his sixteen matches, fifteen being singles.

9. Between 1968 and 1973, the USA won every tie before being defeated at home 5 – 0 by Australia in the final at the end of 1973.

10. Anne Kremer of Luxembourg holds the record for the most appearances in the Fed Cup with 74 appearances. She has 61 wins from 118 matches.

11. Arantxa Sanchez Vicario and Conchita Martinez combined for Spain to win ten Fed Cups.

12. Since the World Group of the Fed Cup started, nine players have had a 100% season. The most recent was in 2017, by US player Coco Vandweghe with 8 – 0.

13. Neale Fraser said of Lew Hoad when he learnt of his death: "He was the first of the charismatic players we saw in the 50s. He produced a brand of tennis that was exciting, different to everyone else, and a joy to watch."

14. At 6 feet 3 inches, Pancho Gonzales was an imposing figure on and off the court. Some players even joked that they lost to him out of fright.

15. One of the few GB successes in the Wightman Cup was in 1968 when sisters Christine and Nell Truman teamed up to win the deciding rubber.

16. Bobby Riggs won all three Wimbledon titles in 1939, and the US singles as well.

17. Bobby Riggs, a professional in the Kramer era, challenged Margaret Court to a "battle of the sexes" in 1973 and beat her comfortably even though he was in his mid-50s. His challenge to Billie Jean King later in the year had a different outcome; 6 – 4, 6 – 3, 6 – 3 in front of 30,000 spectators.

18. Budge Patty spent ten years in the World Top 10, winning 46 singles titles including the French and Wimbledon in 1950 but was perhaps better known for his doubles play. He was 33 and his partner, Gardnar Mulloy, 43 when they won the 1957 Wimbledon doubles.

19. Jaroslav Drobny was born in Czechoslovakia and defected in 1949 while in Switzerland. He took Egyptian citizenship and then applied for British citizenship. Despite having an English wife, he was refused until 1959. He finally won Wimbledon at thirty-two in 1954, the first left-hander for forty years. His last Wimbledon, in 1960, was therefore his first as a Brit.

20. Only one player in the Open Era has won Wimbledon having been given a wildcard; Goran Ivanisevic in 2001.

TRIVIA QUESTIONS

1. What nationality was Drobny when he won Wimbledon?

    A. Russian
    B. Egyptian
    C. French
    D. German
    E. Polish

2. Who was the prime mover behind the Professional Circuit in 1947?

    A. Jack Kramer
    B. Pancho Gonzales
    C. Tony Trabert
    D. Lew Hoad
    E. Rod Laves

3. How many wins did GB have in the history of the Wightman Cup?

    A. 6
    B. 7
    C. 9
    D. 10
    E. 12

4. Who was a regular partner of Arantxa Sanchez Vicario in the Fed Cup?

    A. Martina Navratilova
    B. Jana Novotna
    C. Conchita Martinez
    D. Christine Truman
    E. Anne Kremer

5. Who has won all nine of what are now the ATP Masters events?

    A. Rafa Nadal
    B. Novak Djokovic
    C. Boris Becker
    D. John McEnroe
    E. Ivan Lendl

Answers

1. B
2. A
3. D
4. C
5. E